Confronting & Controlling Thoughts

According to the Fathers of the Philokalia

Anthony M. Coniaris

Third Printing

Light and Life Publishing Company
Minneapolis, Minnesota

Light & Life Publishing Company
Minneapolis, MN
P: (952) 925-3888

Third Printing. 2016

Library of Congress Card No. 2005270924

ISBN No. 1-880971-88-7

TABLE OF CONTENTS

THE INTELLECT OR *NOUS* IN ORTHODOX SPIRITUALITY

Orthodox spirituality places great emphasis on the *nous,* or mind, and the thoughts, *logismoi,* that the mind produces. It does so because everything we do begins in the *nous* or mind with thoughts (*logismoi*). "As a man thinks in his heart, so is he," we read in Proverbs. So, let's begin our study of confronting and controlling thoughts according to the Fathers of the *Philokalia* with a brief study, first of the *nous* (mind), then of the heart, and then move onto the thoughts (*logismoi*) that proceed from the mind and the heart and how the *Philokalia* counsels us to confront and control them.

Most of the Church Fathers we will be consulting on this subject are from the *Philokalia. Philokalia,* as you may know, means "love of the beautiful." It is an anthology of spiritual writings by Church Fathers, ranging from the fourth to the fifteenth century. St. Nicodemus of the Holy Mountain called the *Philokalia*:

> *The treasury of watchfulness, the keeper of the mind, the mystical school of prayer of the heart ... the paradise of the Fathers ... the deep teaching of Christ, the trumpet which calls back the grace ... the instrument itself of deification.*

So, let's look at what these Fathers have to say about the *nous,* mind, the heart and the *logismoi* (thoughts).

NOUS (MIND) IS SPIRITUAL VISION

In an interview, Bishop Kallistos Ware offered the following definition of *nous* or intellect:

> ....Nous, *in particular, is a very difficult word to translate. If you just say "mind,", that is far too vague. In our translation of the* Philokalia, *we, with some hes-*

> *itations, opted for the word intellect, emphasizing that it does not mean primarily the rational faculties. The nous is the spiritual vision that we all possess, though many of us have not discovered it. The nous implies a direct, intuitive appreciation of truth, where we apprehend the truth not simply as the conclusion of a reasoned argument, but we simply see that something is so. The nous is cultivated certainly through study, through training our faculties, but also it is developed through prayer, through fasting, through the whole range of the Christian life. This is what we need to develop most of all as Orthodox, something higher than the reasoning brain and deeper than the emotions.* *1

Nous then is spiritual vision that enables us to recognize truth, as soon as we see it.

An additional definition of *nous* comes from the book *Themes From the Philokalia—The Nous,* Vol. 2.

> *A* nous *that is pure and does not offend God is similar to an eye that does not even accept the smallest dust particle. It is from the* nous *that all the powers of the soul depend. That is why the Lord tells us "if therefore thine eye be single, thy whole body shall be full of light. But if thine eye be evil, thy whole body shall be full of darkness (Matt. 6:22-23). Since the* nous *of contemporary man has fallen into the same sin as Adam and Eve, it has turned towards creation with an unrestrainable idolatrous and evil disposition. In this way the* nous *of man, away from the vision of the glory of God, becomes either demonic or bestial. The* nous *which is overcome by the passions and egoism is unenlightened, dark, short-sighted and feeble.**2

---

*1 From an interview that appeared in the magazine *The Road to Emmaus.* Vol. III, No.3 (#10).

*2 Published by Holy Monastery of St. Gregory Palamas in Thessaloniki, Greece, 1997.

Thus, the purified *nous*, enlightened by God's grace, is designed to be the eye of the soul.

NOUS AS THE *HEGEMONIKON* OR HELM

The *nous* is also designed to preside over the person as the *hegemonikon*, the dominant leader or ruler of the personality. Yet because of the Fall of man, the *nous* has been wounded and is now subject to disruption by *epithymia*, by the desires imposed by the powerful passions. It is only by God's grace and *askesis*, discipline, resistance, that man can be healed and come to prevail over the *epithymia* (desire) of the passions through the power of the Holy Spirit. St. Hesychios states that the Fathers liken the intellect (*nous*) to the leadership of Moses:

> *The Fathers regard Moses the Lawgiver as an ikon of the intellect. He saw God in the burning bush (cf Exod. 3:2-4:17); his face shone with glory (cf. Exod 34:30); he was made a god to Pharaoh by the God of gods (cf. Exod. 7:1); he flayed Egypt with a scourge; he led Israel out of bondage and gave laws. These happenings, when seen metaphorically and spiritually, are activities and privileges of the intellect hegemonikon.*

Like Moses, the *nous* (intellect) is called and empowered by God's grace to be the dominant factor –the acropolis—ruling over the kingdom of self. It is the *hegemonikon,* the rudder that steers and directs the kingdom of self. If the individual person allowed the *hegemonikon* to rule, spiritual harmony and progress would follow. The *hegemonikon* is what Jesus calls "the eye," which, if it is single, will fill the whole body with light (Matt. 6:22-23). Some consider the *hegemonikon* to be the "mind of Christ" which we receive when we "put on Christ" in Holy Baptism.

The translators of the *Philokalia* themselves offer the following definition of *nous* (intellect):

> *(Nous is) …the highest faculty in man, through which – provided it is purified – he knows God….Unlike the* dianoia *or reason from which it must be carefully distinguished, the intellect does not function by formulating abstract concepts and then arguing on this basis to a conclusion reached through deductive reasoning, but it understands divine truth by means of immediate experience, intuition or "simple cognition" (the term used by St. Isaac the Syrian). The intellect dwells in the "depths of the soul"; it constitutes the innermost aspect of the heart….The intellect is the organ of contemplation, the 'eye of the heart' (*Makarian Homilies*).* *

THE *NOUS* (INTELLECT) IS NOT PRESENT IN EVERYONE

St. Anthony the Great tells us that the intellect (*nous*) is not present in everyone:

> *God has ordained that the soul should be filled with intellect as the body grows, so that man may choose from good and evil what conforms to God. A soul which does not choose the good has no intellect. Hence, all bodies have souls, but not every soul has intellect. An intellect enjoying the love of God is present in the self-controlled, the holy, the just, the pure, the good, the merciful and the devout. The presence of intellect helps a man toward God…. The intellect is not present in every soul; and so not every soul is saved…. The intellect in a pure, devout soul truly sees God the unbegotten, invisible and ineffable, who is the sole purity in the pure heart.*

**The Philokalia.* Volume One, Faber and Faber. London, 1979.

THE INTELLECT IS A GIFT THAT SAVES THE SOUL

St. Anthony differentiates between the soul and the intellect (*nous*) which he says are not the same:

> *The intellect is not the soul, but a gift of God that saves the soul; and the intellect that conforms to God goes on ahead of the soul and counsels it to despise what is transitory, material and corruptible, and to turn all its desire towards eternal, incorruptible and immaterial blessings. And the intellect teaches man while still in the body to perceive and contemplate divine and heavenly realities, and everything else as well, through itself. Thus, the intellect that enjoys the love of God is the benefactor and saviour of the human soul.*

THE PURIFIED INTELLECT IS THE SPIRITUAL EYE

St. Gregory of Sinai calls the intellect (*nous*) a spiritual eye as does Jesus in Matt. 6:22-23:

> *The physical eye perceives the outward or literal sense of things and from it derives sensory images. The intellect, once purified and re-established in its pristine state, perceives God and from Him derives divine images. Instead of a book the intellect has the Spirit; instead of a pen, (it has) mind and tongue – "my tongue is a pen," says the Psalmist (cf. Ps. 45:1); and instead of ink,(it has) light. So plunging the mind into the light that it becomes light, the intellect, guided by the Spirit, inscribes the inner meaning of things in the pure hearts of those who listen. Then it grasps the significance of the statement that the faithful "shall be taught by God" (cf. Isa. 54:13; John 6:45), and that through the Spirit God "teaches man knowledge" (Ps. 94:10).*

"The intellect," says St. Gregory, "once purified...perceives God and from Him receives divine images (thoughts)."

MORE COMMENTS BY CHURCH FATHERS ON THE INTELLECT

Following are more comments by various other Fathers of the *Philokalia* as they describe the intellect or *nous.* St. Maximus, the Confessor describes the intellect as that which has the power to choose:

> *Our intellect lies between angel and demon, each of which works for its own ends, the one encouraging virtue and the other vice. The intellect has both the authority and the power to follow or resist whichever it wishes to.*

St. Maximus also calls the intellect "...the organ of wisdom and spiritual knowledge."

Nikitas Stithatos describes further how the intellect functions as an organ of wisdom:

> *If your intellect clearly distinguishes the intentions of its thoughts and in its purity gives its assent only to those that are divine...then through the light of the Sun of righteousness you have transcended all sense-perception and have attained what lies beyond it, and you savour the delight of things unseen.*

St. Thalassios, another one of the *Philokalia* Fathers, teaches that the intellect (*nous*) can subdue the passions:

> *A wise intellect (nous) restrains the soul, keeps the body in subjection, and makes the passions its servants.*

A "wise" intellect, of course, is one that is God-controlled and filled with God's Spirit. St. Peter of Damaskos associates the intellect (*nous*) with the image of God in us:

We should look on man with wonder, conscious that his intellect (nous)*...is the image of God.*

St. Basil extols the intellect (*nous*) as a treasure-house:

> *The mind like a treasure-house tirelessly stores all thoughts. And these thoughts, whether new or long held in store, the intellect when it wishes can express in language; yet although words are always coming from it, it is never exhausted.*

The intellect (*nous*) is constantly working, producing thoughts. It can store an endless number of memories.

St. Thalassios tells us that the task of the *nous* resembles that of a gardener weeding his garden:

> *The intellect's task is to reject any thought that secretly vilifies a fellow being. Just as the gardener who does not weed his garden chokes his vegetables, so the intellect that does not purify its thoughts is wasting its efforts.*

Thus the intellect needs constant attention, weeding out evil thoughts and concentrating on that which is holy, noble and Godly. St. Maximus the Confessor describes the intellect as that which helps us "discriminate":

> *The intellect has the power to discriminate between the spiritual and the sensible, between the eternal and the transitory. Or rather, as the soul's discriminatory power, the intellect persuades the soul to cleave to the first (the spiritual) and to transcend the second (the transitory).*

St. Maximus the Confessor describes how the body is ruled by two laws, that of the flesh and that of the Spirit through the intellect (*nous*):

> *Since man is composed of body and soul, he is moved by two laws, that of the flesh and that of the Spirit (cf. Rom. 7:23). The law of the flesh operates by virtue of the senses; the law of the Spirit operates by virtue of the intellect. The first law, operating by virtue of the senses, automatically binds one closely to matter; the second law, operating by virtue of the intellect, brings about direct union with God. Suppose there is someone who does not doubt in his heart (cf. Mark 11:23) – that is to say, who does not dispute in his intellect – and through such doubt sever that immediate union with God which has been brought about by faith, but who is dispassionate or, rather, has already become god through union with God by faith: then it is quite natural that if such a person says to a mountain, "Go to another place," it will go (cf. Matt. 17:220). The mountain here indicates the will and the law of the flesh, which is ponderous and hard to shift, and in fact, so far as our natural powers are concerned, is totally immovable and unshakeable.*

Man, says St. Maximus is moved by two laws: first, the law of the flesh which drags him down to the animal level; secondly, by the law of the Spirit, which operates through the intellect and helps man ascend to God by grace. It is the law of the Spirit operating through the *nous*, the intellect, that can move the immovable and unshakeable mountains of the passions and unite us to God, says Maximus.

St. Thalassios, echoing the words of Jesus, "Physician, heal thyself," says of the intellect:

> *The truly physician-like intellect is one that first heals itself and then heals others of the diseases of which it has been cured.*

In other words, the *nous* removes first the log from its own eye in order to better see the speck in his brother's eye.

The intellect (*nous*) acquires knowledge of God and discernment by God's grace not by nature. St. Maximus explains:

> *A man whose intellect has been formed by the knowledge that comes by dint of the virtues through the divine Spirit is said to experience divine things; for he has acquired such knowledge not by nature, thanks simply to his existence, but by grace, thanks to his participation in it. When a man has not received knowledge by grace, even though he calls a particular thing spiritual, he does not know its true character from experience. For mere learning does not produce a state of spiritual knowledge.*

Maximus goes on to explain that the intellect does not have the power to ascend to God unless God takes the initiative to elevate it:

> *A soul can never attain the knowledge of God unless God Himself in His condescension takes hold of it and raises it up to Himself. For the human intellect lacks the power to ascend and to participate in divine illumination, unless God Himself draws it up – in so far as this is possible for the human intellect – and illumines it with rays of divine light.*

And to show how God works in synergy with man, Maximus explains that even the Holy Spirit cannot impart wisdom to man unless the intellect is ready to receive it:

> *Not even the grace of the Holy Spirit can actualize wisdom in the saints unless there is an intellect capable of receiving it; or spiritual knowledge unless there is a faculty of intelligence that can receive it; or faith unless there is in the intellect and the intelligence, full assurance about the realities to be disclosed hereafter and until then hidden from everyone… a man cannot acquire a single one of these gifts with his natural faculties unless aided by the divine power that bestows them.*

When faith opens the door to God, says Maximus, it is the intellect (*nous*) that serves as the chalice that receives the gifts of God's wisdom, power and love. Nikitas Stithatos extols the intellect as the organ that moves us toward God and immortality:

> *The glory of the intellect is its power of ascent, its constant movement upwards, its acuity, purity, understanding, wisdom and immortality. The dignity of the intellect lies in its intelligence, its royal sovereign nature, and its power of self-determination…. The intellect's being in the likeness of God resides in its justice, truthfulness, love, sympathy and compassion. When these qualities are energized and guarded in a person, that which is in the image and likeness of God is clearly manifest in him.*

THE INTELLECT IN SUMMARY

In summary, here is what the Fathers of the *Philokalia* teach about the intellect (*nous*):

- The intellect (*nous*) is the spiritual vision of God we possess through Baptism though this vision is undiscovered by some. We must remember that when we are baptized, we are clothed with Christ. We put on "the mind of Christ."

- The intellect implies a direct, intuitive recognition of truth as something that is so. It's as if a light suddenly goes on and we recognize the truth in all its splendor.
- The intellect is developed and cultivated through the study of God's Word, through prayer and the sacraments.
- "The purified intellect (*nous*) understands divine truth by immediate experience, intuition or simple cognition," write the translators of the *Philokalia*.
- The *nous* is the benefactor and savior of the soul (St. Anthony).
- The *nous* is described by Jesus as the eye that is "...the lamp of the body. If therefore your eye is good, your whole body will be full of light. But if your eye is bad, your whole body will be full of darkness. If therefore the light in you is darkness, how great is that darkness" (Matt. 6:22-23).
- The purified intellect (*nous*) is a spiritual eye that serves as a lamp filling the body with a light. But if the eye is "bad," i.e., not functioning, the body is filled with darkness.
- The *nous* is called and empowered to be by God's grace the *hegemonikon*, the rudder or helm that steers and rules the kingdom of self.
- The *nous* is the highest faculty in man through which, if purified, we come to know God.
- "The intellect enjoys the love of God and is present in the self-controlled, the holy, the just, the pure, the good, the merciful and the devout" (St. Anthony).
- "A soul which does not choose the good has no intellect.... The intellect is not present in every

soul; and so not every soul is saved" (St. Anthony).

- "The intellect (*nous*) is not the soul, but a gift of God that saves the soul. It counsels the soul to despise what is transitory...and to turn all its desire towards God" (St. Anthony).
- "The intellect is the organ of wisdom and spiritual knowledge" (St. Maximus).
- "A wise intellect makes the passions its servants" (St. Thalassios).
- "The intellect is the image of God" (St. Peter of Damaskos).
- The intellect is the organ of contemplation.
- It is the "eye of the heart" (Macarius).
- The intellect is "a treasure-house that tirelessly stores all thoughts" (St. Basil).
- Just as a gardener weeds his garden, so the intellect is called to reject evil thoughts in order that the flowers of virtue may grow (St. Thalassios).
- The purified intellect has the power to discriminate between good and bad thoughts (St. Maximus).
- Man is ruled either by the law of the flesh or the law of the Spirit. The law of the Spirit operates through the intellect (St. Maximus).
- The intellect acquires knowledge of God and the gift of discernment only by God's grace, aided by prayer, the sacraments and the study of God's Word.
- The glory of the intellect is its power of ascent, its constant movement upwards toward God; its movement towards justice; truthfulness, love, sympathy, and compassion (Nikitas Stithatos).

ST. PAUL ON THE LAW OF THE MIND AND THE LAW OF THE FLESH

Let us ponder for a moment what St. Paul says about the law of the mind (*nous*) and the law of the flesh. He describes how both these laws operated within him:

> *For I delight in the law of God according to the inward man. But I see another law in my members, warring against the law of my mind, and bringing me into captivity to the law of sin which is in my members. O wretched man that I am! Who will deliver me from this body of death? I thank God – through Jesus Christ our Lord! So then, with the mind I myself serve the law of God, but with the flesh, the law of sin (Rom. 7:22-25).*

St. Diodochus of Photike comments on the battle between the intellect (*nous*) and the flesh that St. Paul described above:

> *How can St. Paul say that "with my intellect I serve the law of God, but with the flesh the law of sin" (Rom. 7:25), unless the intellect is completely free to engage in battle with the demons, gladly submitting itself to grace, whereas the body is attracted by the smell of mindless pleasures? He can only say this because the wicked spirits of deception are free to lurk in the bodies of those pursuing a spiritual way; "for I know that in me – that is, in my flesh – there dwells nothing good" (Rom. 7:18), says the Apostle, referring to those who are resisting and struggling against sin. Here he is not merely expressing a personal opinion. The demons attack the intellect, but they do so by trying through lascivious temptations to entice the flesh down the slope of sensual pleasure. It is for a good purpose that the*

demons are allowed to dwell within the body even of those who are struggling vigorously against sin; for in this way man's free will is constantly put to the test. If a man, while still alive, can undergo death through his labours, then in his entirety he becomes the dwelling-place of the Holy Spirit; for such a man, before he has died, has already risen from the dead, as was the case with the blessed Apostle Paul and all those who have struggled and are struggling to the utmost against sin.

The law of the flesh drags us down. The law of the mind through faith and by God's grace raises us from the dead and makes us living temples of the Holy Spirit.

WHERE DOES THE INTELLECT ABIDE?

St. Gregory Palamas asks the question, "What organs does the power of the soul that we call intellect make use of when it is active?" In other words, where in the body does the *nous* dwell? He answers as follows:

No one has ever supposed that the mind resides in the finger-nails or the eye-lashes, the nostrils or the lips. But we all agree that it resides within us, even though we may not all agree as to which of our inner organs it chiefly makes use of. For some locate it in the head, as though in a sort of acropolis; others consider that its vehicle is the centermost part of the heart, that aspect of the heart that has been purified.... We know very well that our intelligence is neither within us as in a container... – nor yet outside us, for it is united to us; but it is located in the heart as in its own organ. And we know this because we are taught it not by men but by the Creator of man Himself when He says, "It is not that which goes into man's mouth that defiles him, but what comes out of it" (Matt. 15:11), adding, "for

> *thoughts come out of the heart" (Matt. 15:19). St. Makarios the Great says the same: "The heart rules over the whole human organism, and when grace takes possession of the pastures of the heart, it reigns over all a man's thoughts and members. For the intellect and all the thoughts of the soul are located there."*
>
> *Our heart is, therefore, the shrine of the intelligence and the chief intellectual organ of the body. When, therefore, we strive to scrutinize and to amend our intelligence through rigorous watchfulness, how could we do this if we did not collect our intellect, outwardly dispersed through the senses, and bring it back within ourselves – back to the heart itself, the shrine of the thoughts? It is for this reason that St. Makarios – rightly called blessed – directly after what he says above, adds: "So it is there that we must look to see whether grace has inscribed the laws of the Spirit." Where? In the ruling organ, in the throne of grace, where the intellect and all the thoughts of the soul reside, that is to say, in the heart. Do you see, then, how greatly necessary it is for those who have chosen a life of self-attentiveness and stillness to bring their intellect back and to enclose it within their body, and particularly within that innermost body within the body that we call the heart?*

Thus, when St. Paul says in Romans 10:9 that it is with the heart that one believes, he includes the *nous* or intellect which dwells in the heart (Rom. 10:9). This is why many spiritual writers include the *nous* in the heart by combining the two words and speaking of the "mind-heart."

DESCEND WITH THE MIND INTO THE HEART

For this reason the Fathers of the *Philokalia* urge us when we pray, "to descend with the mind into the heart." How? St.

Nikiphoros urges us to descend with the mind into the heart through the Jesus Prayer:

> *When your intellect is firmly established in your heart, it must not remain there silent and idle; it should constantly repeat and meditate on the prayer, "Lord Jesus Christ, Son of God, have mercy on me," and should never stop doing this. For this prayer protects the intellect from distraction, renders it impregnable to diabolic attacks, and every day increases its love and desire for God.*

Bishop Ignatii teaches that descending with the mind into the heart helps us grow in discernment:

> *Do you wish to grow wise in discernment of thoughts? Descend from the head into the heart. Then you will see all thoughts clearly, as they move before the eye of your sharp-sighted mind. But until you descend into the heart, do not expect to have due discrimination of thoughts.*

A UNION OF MIND AND HEART

The over-intellectual scholars in Constantinople criticized St. Gregory Palamas and his way of prayer. Faith to them was only a matter of the mind not of the heart. For Gregory Palamas it was both. It was the mind in the heart. And the Church supported his view.

St. Theophan writes:

> *You must descend with your mind into your heart. At present your thoughts of God are in your head. And God Himself is, as it were, outside you, and so your prayer and other spiritual exercises remain exterior. Whilst you are still in your head, thoughts*

will...always be whirling about like snow in winter, or clouds of mosquitoes in the summer.... All our inner disorder is due to the dislocation of our powers, the mind and the heart each going its own way. The mind must come to an initial concord with the heart, growing eventually into a union of the mind with the heart.

Thus it is that the Fathers of the *Philokalia* invite us through prayer to dive into the fathomless depths of the heart with the *nous,* into "the Lord's reception room," there to discover the kingdom of God.

DESCENDING WITH THE MIND INTO THE HEART THROUGH THE JESUS PRAYER

The Fathers of the *Philokalia* urge us to lead the mind from the head into the heart by praying the Jesus Prayer, "Lord Jesus, Son of God, have mercy on me." In praying the Jesus Prayer, St. Nikiphoros recommends that the intellect (*nous*) descend by way of the Jesus Prayer into the heart so that the mind and the heart are united. He describes the effect of this as "a sense of joyful homecoming like that of a man long absent from abroad, who cannot restrain his gladness at once more meeting his wife and children." Thus, St. Theophan the Recluse admonishes:

Make yourself a rule always to be with the Lord, keeping your mind in your heart, and do not let your thoughts wander; as often as they stray, turn them back again and keep them at home in the closet of your heart, and delight in converse with the Lord.

And we do this by praying the Jesus Prayer. Once the mind descends into the heart, the mind-heart becomes illuminated and empowered by the flame of the Holy Spirit. If the *nous,* which is the lamp of the body is good, pure and Christ-centered, the whole body will be full of light.

MORE ON DESCENDING WITH THE MIND INTO THE HEART

St. Theophan the Recluse defines prayer as "standing before God with the mind in the heart."

Bishop Kallistos Ware explains what these words mean:

> *So long as the ascetic prays with the mind in the head, he will still be working solely with the resources of the human intellect, and on this level he will never attain to an immediate and personal encounter with God. By the use of his brain, he will at best know* about *God, but he will not* know *God. For there can be no direct knowledge of God without an exceedingly great love, and such love must come, not from the brain alone, but from the whole man – that is, from the heart. It is necessary, then, for the ascetic to descend from the head into the heart. He is not required to abandon his intellectual powers – reason, too, is a gift of God – but he is called to descend* with the mind *into his heart."* *

A HEAD-IN-THE-HEART FAITH

The head seeks God but it is the heart that finds Him. "For man believes in his heart and so is justified…" writes St. Paul (Romans 10:10). When the head descends into the heart, the *head* faith becomes a *heart* faith. It becomes not just a *head* faith or just a *heart* faith but a *head-in-the-heart* faith. Just as love, charity and the other important virtues cannot exist only in the mind but are primarily of the heart, so it is with our faith and trust in God. We are not to let Jesus remain in the mind and give Him only a cold intellectual allegiance. He must descend into the heart where we shall be able to feel His presence, yield our will to

*"*The Art of Prayer*" compiled by Igumen Chariton. Faber and Faber Ltd. London. 1966.

Him, and love Him with all our mind and heart.

To return again to St. Theophan the Recluse:

> *You must pray not only with words but with the mind, and not only with the mind but with the heart, so that the mind understands and sees-clearly what is said in words, and the heart feels what the mind is thinking. All these combined together constitute real prayer, and if any of them are absent, your prayer is either not perfect, or it is not prayer at all.*

St. John Chrysostom says that God hears our prayers more loudly when we are praying with the mind in the heart.

WHEN WE THINK WE ARE PRAYING

St. John of Kronstadt talks about people who "call prayer that which is not prayer at all: for instance, a man goes to church, stands there for a time, looks at the icons or at other people, and says that he has prayed to God; or else he stands before an icon at home, bows his head, says some words he has learned by heart, without understanding, and without feeling, and says that he has prayed—although with his thoughts and his heart he has not prayed at all, but was elsewhere, with other people and other things, and not with God."

He goes on to say, "Thus he who does not pray with his heart does not pray at all, because only his body prays, and the body without the mind is nothing more than dust." That is why St. Theophan encourages us to descend with the head into the heart:

> *Do not be lazy about descending. In the heart is life, and you must live there. Do not think that this is something to be attempted only by the perfect. No, it is for everyone who has begun to seek the Lord.*

THE JOURNEY WITHIN

By descending with the mind into the heart through prayer, the Church is calling on us to make what someone called "the longest journey, the journey inward" to the center of our being which is nothing other than the Presence of God within the heart, "the Lord's reception room."

So dive into prayer often. Let the words of prayer be on your lips. Let them go from your lips to your mind to your heart. Let your heart be without words but never your words without heart. As you so pray, the strengthening presence of Jesus will be with you. The healing love of Jesus will be poured upon you. The resurrecting power of Jesus will flow through you to touch, bless and heal your mind, soul and body.

Many centuries ago Augustine observed, "Indeed, how can we worthily praise with our tongue Him Whom we cannot yet see in our heart? There it is that He has placed the eye with which He can be seen."

THE HEART

Let us now look briefly at what the Bible and the Fathers say about the heart. The heart is one of the greatest gifts God has given us. If the heart is right with God, the whole person is filled with light. If the heart is bad, the whole person is filled with darkness and "how great is the darkness," said Jesus. St. Macarios of Egypt put it this way:

> *The heart governs the whole body and when God's grace possesses the heart, then it reigns over all thoughts. This is so because the heart is the place where the mind and the thoughts are found.*

THE FACULTIES OF THE HEART

The intellect (*nous*) is included in the heart, yet the heart is much greater than the *nous*. In addition to the intellect by which we know God, the heart includes volition, the will to choose to follow God's commandments.

> *God endowed our free will with such power that even if all a man's faculties, the whole world and all the demons rose up in arms against him and attacked him, they could not compel it. It is always left free to desire what they offer or demand, if it so wishes, or not to desire it, if it does not wish (Unseen Warfare).*

The heart also includes the faculty of loving and desiring God. Thus, the three faculties of the heart are designed to know God with the *nous*; to love God with the heart; and to choose freely (volition) to follow Him. St. Maximus expressed it this way:

> *The mind's aim is to have knowledge of God. The sensation's aim is to desire and love God, and the volition's aim is the will to do what God commands.*

This is why the heart is greater than the intellect (mind) since it includes the intellect plus the sensation of desire and love, plus volition, free will, through which we freely choose to obey God. St. Nicodemos of the Holy Mountain explained this further by using the example of a wheel with spokes:

> *We must therefore keep in mind that as the center of a wagon wheel has a certain number of spokes going out to the circumference of the circle and returning to the center where they meet, so also is the heart of man like a center where all the senses, all the powers of the body, and all the activities of the soul are united.*

"When the mind is in the heart such as it should be according to its nature, then the whole of the soul is one virtue," wrote St. Anthony (c. 251-356). This is what the saints describe as having "the mind of Christ" which St. Hesychios (d. 432) describes as follows, "The mind when it becomes purified, looks up to God and receives divine knowledge from Him. Then it understands the words: 'They shall be all taught of God'" (John 6:45).

THE HEART IS THE COMMAND CENTER

Just as our physical heart controls most of the functions of the body, so our spiritual heart is the center of all that we think, say, love, hate, choose and do in life. Archimandrite Spyridon Logothetis emphasized the importance of the two hearts, the physical and the spiritual, when he wrote:

> *Every man has two hearts. One is the body's heart. The other is the soul's heart. The good or bad condition of both of our hearts is very important. If something happens to either one, then we have heart problems and our life is in danger, whether it is the life of our body or the life of our soul.* *

Fr. Logothetis goes on to say that just as the petroleum that rises to the surface from the depths of the earth needs to be refined, so the thoughts that rise from the depths of the heart need to be filtered and purified once they reach the surface (*nous*). Thus, the heart which the Fathers call "the Lord's reception room" can also be the abode of evil and sin; what psychiatrists call the unconscious; the place that St. Paul describes so well when he talks about the law of the flesh within him warring against the law of the mind. The same heart into which God

**The Heart.* Archimandrite Spyridon Logothetis. Holy Transfiguration Monastery. Nafpaktos, Greece. 2001.

pours His love through the Holy Spirit, "God has poured out His love into our hearts by the Holy Spirit, whom He has given us" (Rom. 5:5), this same heart can also be the abode of demons.

THE CONSCIOUS MIND / THE UNCONSCIOUS HEART

The heart may be compared to the unconscious that plays an important role in contemporary psychiatry and psychology. In the heart, or the unconscious, are buried all the things we ever did (now forgotten) as well as all the passions we have inherited. Jesus spoke specifically to this truth when He said, "Out of the heart," the unconscious, "proceed evil thoughts, adulteries, murders....the things which defile a person" (Mark 7:21-23). Yet out of the same unconscious mind, buried in the heart, we have also inherited many good things as well, such as the voice of conscience, the knowledge of God, a sense of right and wrong, etc.

> *In creating man, God implanted in him a thought which illumines the mind and shows what is good and what bad. This is called conscience, and it is a natural law. By following this law, conscience, the patriarchs and all the saints pleased God, even before the Law was written. – Dorotheus*

THE STRUGGLE BETWEEN THE CONSCIOUS MIND AND THE UNCONSCIOUS HEART

A problem arises when the thoughts of the conscious mind are at odds with the desires of the heart, the unconscious. As St. Paul so well expressed it in Romans 7:22-25, when the conscious mind wants to obey God, and the heart objects, a great struggle takes place between the mind and the heart, the conscious and the unconscious. In this struggle St. Paul describes from personal experience how the thoughts of the heart, i.e., the passions are stronger than the thoughts of the conscious mind to the point where they overrule them.

Dee Pennock, a noted Orthodox writer, described this inner struggle with the passions:

> *When our conscious mind wants to change us for the better in some way, all the passions packed in our unconscious mind, our heart, are saying, "Not on your life!" They're taking the steering wheel and heading in the opposite direction. At that point, instead of giving up on our wonderful will, what we have to do, with God's help, is tackle those passions that are trying to grab the wheel, and regain control of our own steering mechanism.**

This was the experience of St. Paul when he cried out, "Who will deliver me from this body of death?" Through prayer he overcame the passions that were trying to de-rail him, and he was able to proclaim, "I thank God through Jesus Christ our Lord" (Rom.7:24-25).

FILL THE VACUUM WITH GOD

Jesus warned that when the heart is left empty after a demon has been expelled, then that same demon will go back and take seven other demons with him, even more wicked than himself—they enter and dwell there and the last state of that person's heart is worse than it was at first (Matt. 12:43-45). It is not only nature that loves a vacuum, Satan also rejoices when he sees a vacuum. He moves in and takes over. Not so when God is present in the heart. Then Satan flees. St. Gregory Palamas pointed out the danger of inner emptiness, "Thus when God's grace does not dwell in man, then the demons make a nest at the bottom of man's heart, like real snakes, and they never permit the heart of man to desire the good."

**The Adam Complex: The Passions of Adam and Eve.* Dee Pennock. Light and Life Publishing Company. Minneapolis, MN. 2004.

THE IMPORTANCE OF THE HEART

Satan strives to invade the heart through temptation. There—in the heart—sin is born, and there—in the heart—hell begins. That is why many people walk around with a portable hell in their hearts. In the words of St. Basil:

> *The heart's decision is the root of the body's activities. This is so because adultery first lights like a fire in the heart of a sensual man and then creates a sinful corruption of the body—by committing adultery.*

And that is why Jesus said, "Anyone who looks at a woman lustfully has already committed adultery with her in his heart" (Matt. 5:27-28). "For out of the heart proceed evil thoughts, murders, adulteries, fornications, thefts, false witnesses, blasphemies" (Matt. 15:19). Elsewhere Jesus said, "No good tree bears bad fruit, nor does a bad tree bear good fruit. Each tree is recognized by its own fruit. People do not pick figs from thornbushes nor grapes from briers. In this exact way, the good man brings offerings from the good treasure of his heart's goodness, and the evil man offers evil things from the evil stored up in his heart. For out of the overflow of his heart his mouth speaks" (Luke 6: 43-45).

How much we need to make the psalmist's prayer our own prayer each and every day, "Create in me a clean heart, O God" (Psalm 51:10).

"MY SON, GIVE ME YOUR HEART"

"My son, give me your heart," says the Lord (Prov. 23:26). God wants our heart. He wants it as His throne. He desires to reign there, to preside and rule as king. "For where your treasure is, there will your heart be also," said Jesus (Matt. 6:21). There is not room enough for two kings on the throne of the heart, only one. God and mammon cannot both sit on the same throne.

THE HEART AS THE CENTER OF OUR BEING

The heart is not only the center of one's being; it is also everything that a person is. Thus, St. Theophan the Recluse describes the heart as the place of God's presence:

> *The heart is the innermost man, or spirit. Here are located self-awareness, the conscience, the idea of God and of one's dependence on him, and all the eternal treasures of the spiritual life.... The physical heart is a piece of muscular flesh, but it is not the flesh that feels, but the soul; the carnal heart serves as an instrument for these feelings, just as the brain serves as an instrument for the mind. Stand in the heart, with the faith that God is also there.* *

Philip Sherrard, the noted Orthodox philosopher and religious writer (as well as one of the translators of the *Philokalia*) defines the position of the heart in Orthodox anthropology as:

> *The receptacle of grace, the "place" of the presence of divine life, is where we encounter God and in union with God become integrated and transfigured beings. The art of the spiritual life is therefore to become conscious of the "treasure hidden in the heart" – to become conscious of the real but unapprehended presence of God in the heart; and this art is effectuated by inducing the intellect, freed from extraneous thoughts and images, to "descend" into the heart and so to become conscious of the divine presence hidden there.**

Our task is to become "conscious of the treasure hidden in the heart." What is the "treasure hidden in the heart?" "Christ, the hope of glory." We are called to descend there with the mind through prayer to stand in the presence of God. One of the most insightful descriptions of the mystery of the heart was given by St. Macarios:

*Within the heart there are unfathomable depths. There are reception rooms and bedchambers in it, doors and porches, and many offices and passages. In it is the workshop of righteousness and of wickedness. In it is death; in it is life.... The heart is Christ's palace: there Christ the King comes to take rest, with angels and the spirit of the saints, and He dwells there, walking within it and placing His Kingdom there.**

Metropolitan Anthony Bloom invites us to journey within the heart to discover there the presence of God:

St. John Chrysostom said, "Find the door of the inner chamber of your soul and you will discover that this is the door into the kingdom of Heaven." St. Ephraim of Syria says that God, when He created man, put in the deepest part of him all the kingdom, and that the problem of human life is to dig deep enough to come upon the hidden treasure. Therefore, to find God we must dig in search of this inner chamber, of this place where the whole kingdom of God is present at the very core of us, where God and we can meet. The best tool, the one which will go through all obstacles, is prayer. The problem is one of praying attentively, simply and truthfully....

Thus, to repeat the words of St. Theophan: just as the physical brain is the instrument used by the *nous*, or mind, to know God, so the physical heart, the heart of flesh and blood, is the instrument through which we come to love God. So, says Theophan, "Stand in the heart, with the faith that God is there

---

*1 *The Art of Prayer* compiled by Chariton. Faber and Faber. London,1966.
*2 *Christianity and Eros.* Philip Sherrard. Denise Harvey Publ. Evia, Greece, 2002.
*3 *The Art of Prayer.* Compiled by Igumen Chariton. Faber and Faber. London, 1966.

also." For this we need a pure heart. So we pray with the psalmist, "Create a clean heart in me, O God" (Psalm 51).

LOGISMOS OR THOUGHT: PRECURSOR OF PASSIONS

The Fathers of the *Philokalia* define *logismos* as follows:

> *Logismos frequently signifies not thought in the ordinary sense, but thought provoked by the demons, and therefore (the word is) often qualified in translation by the adjective "evil" or "demonic"; it can also signify divinely-inspired thought.*

St. Gregory of Sinai describes such evil thoughts as "precursors of the passions":

> *Distractive thoughts are the promptings of the demons and precursors of the passions, just as such promptings and mental images are also the precursors of particular actions. There can be no action either for good or evil, that is not initially provoked by the particular thought of that action; for thought is the impulse... that provokes us to act at all, whatever the action may be.*

In other words, "As a man thinks in his heart, so is he." "No passion is born without a thought" (Mark the Ascetic). St. Ephraim the Syrian compares these *logismoi* to waves constantly beating against ocean rocks:

> *Just as it is natural for ocean rocks to be pounded by waves, similarly man will undoubtedly come into contact with the assaults borne of thoughts.*

THE STRATEGY OF THE EVIL ONE

The devil follows a pattern when he comes to tempt us with thoughts (*logismoi*). First he tries to set us at ease. He begins by assuring us that there is nothing wrong with committing a certain sin because, after all, God is compassionate and merciful, and will forgive us anyway. But once we have gone ahead and committed the evil deed, Satan plants in us the opposite *logismos*, or thought. He then switches and presents God not as merciful and forgiving, but as a merciless judge who will not forgive us, but will toss us into the eternal fire of damnation. He plants in us the *logismos* that we are no longer worthy to approach God, that even if we do, He will reject us. He closes the door for our return to God and plants in us the seeds of hopelessness and despair. He then plagues us with feelings of unworthiness. Satan is an expert at using thoughts to destroy us. He has thousands of years of experience.

This is the devious strategy Satan uses with us as described by the Church Fathers:

> *[Seduction] is never set forth in its naked deformity, lest, being thus exposed, it should at once be detected. But it is craftily decked out in an attractive dress, so as, by its outward form, to make it appear to the inexperienced, ridiculous as the expression may seem, more true than the truth itself. – Irenaeus*

St. Anthony adds:

> *The devil usually hides his gall under an appearance of sweetness, so as to avoid detection; and he fabricates illusions, beautiful to look at, which in reality are not at all what they seem – to seduce your heart by a cunning imitation of truth and goodness, which is rightly attractive.*

HOW SATAN USES *LOGISMOI* TO STEAL OUR PRAYERS

We read in that spiritual classic, *The Way of the Pilgrim*, of how Satan endeavors to steal our prayers through *logismoi*:

> *My late elder used to say that obstacles to prayer come from two sides, the left and the right; that if the enemy does not succeed in turning us away from prayer by vain and sinful thoughts, then he brings to mind instructive and beautiful thoughts only to turn us away from prayer, which he cannot tolerate. And through this right-handed stealing, the soul abandons its communion with God, turns to its own thoughts, and talks to itself or to creatures. Therefore, he taught me that during prayer I should not succumb even to the most beautiful spiritual thoughts and that, if I discover at the end of the day that more time was spent in edifying thoughts and conversation than in real interior prayer of the heart, I should regard this as intemperance.*

How should we cope with such "right-handed and beautiful" *logismoi* in prayer? St. Theophan recommends the Jesus Prayer as an effective weapon for controlling such *logismoi*. He writes:

> *[Thoughts] continue to jostle in your heard like mosquitoes. To stop this jostling, you must bind the mind with one thought, or the thought of God only. An aid to this is a short prayer, which helps the mind to become simple and united: it develops feeling towards God and is engrafted with it. When this feeling arises within us, the consciousness of the soul becomes established in God, and the soul begins to do everything according to His will. Together with the short prayer, you must keep your thought and attention toward God.*

This one short simple prayer that scatters the mosquitoes and unites the soul in its attentiveness to God is the Jesus Prayer.

YOU ARE WHERE YOUR MIND IS

The Fathers of the *Philokalia* keep emphasizing the importance of guarding the mind so that it is completely present to the task at hand. They keep saying that wherever our mind is, there is where we are, and wherever our mind is not, there is where we are not. A person, for example, may be in church or at home praying, but if his mind is not in his prayer, if, with his mind he is lounging on a beach in Tahiti, 6,000 miles away, then he is not present to God. He is not praying. Wherever our mind is, there is where we are. This happens often in life. Here are a few examples.

The middle-aged businessman seated at the family dinner table is concerned about his need for an operation, about the expenses involved, about the deadlines he must meet before he can take time off from his work, about possible complications following surgery, etc. These concerns pass through his mind to the extent that he is barely conscious of his food or of his loved ones sitting at the same table with him.

His son, eating at the same table, might be thinking about the girl he met between classes. Preoccupied with her, he is completely oblivious of his father and mother eating with him.

His mother sitting next to him at the table, might be worrying about something else that keeps her attention from the family dinner and causes her great anxiety.

None of these persons, although they are members of the same family and sitting at the same table, is present to each other. They are miles away from each other, wrapped up in their own thoughts and fears about tomorrow. Not being really present, they are complete strangers to each other.

One of the worst things we can do to our children as parents is to give them half of our interest because to give them half of our interest is to give them half of ourselves. A half-wit is someone who is only half there.

Wherever our intellect (*nous*) is, there is where we are.

Thus, we are to descend with the mind into the heart not only when speaking to God but also when relating to our loved ones in order to be completely present to them, mind, heart and soul.

THE GREATEST KIND OF LOVE

Suppose you came to me, a priest, at church and I kept glancing at my watch, worrying about my next appointment. You would be deeply hurt by this, because I would not be giving you my full attention. You would be less open than if you had my complete attention that moment. *You* experienced my nervousness, my being in a hurry, my lack of attentiveness as a lack of interest in *you*. And this turns you off completely. So, almost automatically, by being completely present to people, by behaving as if the person who is with us at the moment is the only person who exists, by giving them our undivided attention when we are with them, a relationship can become more real, more loving, and more life-changing.

Being completely present to people may be the greatest kind of love we can give them. For in a strange way, we are giving them our whole attention. Perhaps this is the most real way to value a person as a human being—to really be *with* him and take him seriously as he is. A single such contact may change the whole direction of a life. So, descend with the mind into the heart to be completely present not only to God but also to people. It is a great act of love.

THE EXAMPLE OF JESUS

A truly great example of being completely present is our Lord Jesus Christ. He notices Zacchaeus hidden up in a tree and invites him to have dinner with Him. He hears the call of the blind beggar by the roadside and responds with healing. He hears the cry of the penitent thief on the cross and says, "Today, you will be with Me in Paradise."

How often people come to us, children to parents, wives to husbands, friends to friends, trying to unload their burdens, and as we sit there listening, our minds and hearts are thousands of miles away. If we were completely present to each other, we would rightfully expect miracles to happen. To be completely present is to care; it is to love; it is to gain a most precious gift: understanding.

Dr. Paul Tournier in his book *A Doctor's Case-Book* says that sometimes a patient says to him, "I admire the patience with which you listen to everything I tell you." Then he says, "It is not patience at all, it is love, care, concern."

Imagine how God must feel when we come to Him in prayer and we are really not present to Him, having been distracted by *logismoi*. We may be on our knees, we may even be in church, but we allow Satan to steal our prayers by inattentiveness.

True meeting and true dialogue take place only in the present moment when two persons are fully present to each other—mind, heart, soul and body.

This is why the Fathers of the *Philokalia* emphasize so greatly the importance of guarding the intellect from *logismoi*, the distracting thoughts that prevent us from being completely present to God in prayer and to our loved ones when we are in their presence.

Archbishop Anthony Bloom provides a personal example of the importance of being completely present with our mind and heart to the person or task immediately before us.

> *In the beginning, when I was a physician, I felt it was most unfair to the people who were in the waiting room if I was slow in seeing the person who was with me in the consulting room. So the first day I tried to be as quick as I could with those in the consulting room. I discovered by the end of my surgery hours that*

I had not the slightest recollection of the people I had seen, because all the time a patient was with me, I was looking beyond him with clairvoyant eyes into the next room and counting the heads of those who were not with me. The result was that all the questions I asked I had to ask twice, all the examinations I made I had to make twice or even three times. When I had finished, I could not remember whether I had done these things or not. Of course everyone is not like me, you may be able to recollect much better than I, but this is just an example of what may happen even to one of you.

*Then I felt this was simply dishonest, and I decided that I would behave as if the person who was with me was the only one who existed. The moment I began to feel "I must be quick," I would sit back and engage in small talk for a few minutes just to prevent myself from hurrying. I discovered within two days that you no longer need to do anything like that. You can simply be completely concerned with the person or task that is in front of you, and when you have finished, you will discover that you have spent half the time doing it, instead of all the time you took before; yet you have seen everything and heard everything.**

YOU ARE WHAT YOUR THOUGHTS MAKE YOU

The Turkish wit, Nasrettin Hodja, went by a pet shop in his hometown one day and saw a parrot costing one hundred dollars. It was a tiny little bird and he was amazed at the price. Remembering the turkey at home, he brought it to the shop and offered it for sale. "I only want two hundred dollars for it," he said. "Are you mad?" shouted the merchant. "Why," said Hodja, "if that small parrot costs one hundred, then this turkey should be worth at least four hundred." "But," the shopkeeper

**Beginning To Pray*. Anthony Bloom. Paulist Press. New York, 1970.

replied, "the parrot can talk. What can your bird do?" "My bird is a philosopher," said Hodja. "He thinks."

THOUGHTS ARE POWERFUL

Thoughts are powerful. Descartes, the famous philosopher, said, "I think, therefore I am." Marcus Aurelius wrote, "The soul is dyed the color of its thoughts." St. Maximus said, "If you do not first sin in thought, you will never sin in deed." "As a man thinks in his heart, so is he," we read in the Book of Proverbs. We create demons within ourselves by welcoming and entertaining evil thoughts. And we create hell in ourselves by welcoming and entertaining such *logismoi*, evil thoughts. An unknown author wrote "It's the weather in your mind that determines the climate of the day." Change your thoughts and you change not only your life but also your world. You are today where your thoughts have brought you. You will be tomorrow where your thoughts will take you.

Someone quipped, "You may not be what you think you are, but what you think, you are." Another wag said, "People who say, 'I think....' should always make sure they think before they speak." Too many people speak without thinking. A Greek proverb says, "Do not let the tongue run ahead of your mind." Keep the two connected.

Blaise Pascal, the great thinker, said, "Man is obviously made to think. It is his whole dignity and his whole merit; his whole duty is to think as he ought." Yet there is truth in what someone said quite humorously, "Five percent of people think. Ten percent think they think, and the rest would rather die than think." Another person said, "If you don't think too good, then, please, don't think too much."

So powerful are thoughts that Dr. Walter Alvarez of the Mayo Clinic once said, "The sufferings of the mind are more severe than the pains of the body."

A Persian proverb says, "Taking the first step with the good thought, the second step with the good word, and the third step with the good deed, I enter paradise."

It is a truism that what goes in a mind comes out in a life. "Nurture good thoughts for you will never go higher than your thoughts," said Benjamin Disraeli.

FOUR THOUSAND THOUGHTS EACH DAY

Through our thoughts, we are constantly creating. The mind is inventing one thought after another constantly, even as we sleep. But few of us pause long enough to reflect that whatever thought our mind clings to will find expression in life.

Research at the University of Minnesota has revealed that the average human being has about 4000 distinct thoughts in a sixteen-hour day. This means that over a life span of seventy years a person has a total of about one hundred million thoughts. According to the Church Fathers the majority of these thoughts (*logismoi*) are not positive but negative due to our fallen nature.

THE MIND IS A BATTLEFIELD

This is why the mind has been described as a battlefield. All battles are lost or won first in the internal dialogue of the mind. John Milton wrote, "The mind is its own place and in itself can make a heaven of hell, and hell out of heaven."

The famous Coptic Orthodox monk and spiritual mentor, Father Matta El-Maskeen, has written:

> *The mind is the battlefield where man first meets with sin. It is the frontier wherein mankind encounters its grim archenemy, the devil.*
>
> *It is not strange that the enemy should choose man's mind as the battlefield for waging his ferocious struggles. Psychologists say that the mind is the crown atop the human body which directs our actions and behavior whether we are awake or asleep; it controls feelings, awareness, emotions, the will, and thoughts as*

> *well. Thus is man's mind the center that controls human behavior.*
>
> *Therefore if man is defeated in this battlefield, it is the devil that is then in possession of all man's talents and capabilities. Along with this the devil, as we know him, is a mental force with powers that are extraordinary and varied. However, in spite of all this, he still does not have access to us except through our minds. This is an important fact that many of us need to be aware of – especially those struggling in the realm of virtue, righteousness, and chastity. For although the devil is a formidable spiritual power, the sphere of his activity against man is quite limited. He cannot approach anyone except through the mind, the only part of our nature that is susceptible to doing battle with him – the mind is the target of his attacks.*

Drawing from the Eastern Fathers of the *Philokalia,* Fr. George Timko wrote:

> *The Fathers always stress that the chief delusion of man is that he thinks his body is making him sin. He blames his body all the time. If lust awakens in him, he says, "That is a God-given thing in my human nature." He thinks that lust originates with his sexual hormones and not with his mind. But the body is a neutral instrument, say the Fathers; don't blame it. If you want to discover the source of sin, you had better start looking at your mind. According to Mark the Ascetic, "Having sinned, blame your mind and not your body. For if the mind had not run on ahead into sin, the body would not have followed."* *

*"*Speaking of Silence."* Edited by Susan Walker. Paulist Press, NY. 1987, p. 179.

Evagrius, an early Church Father, agrees that it is in the mind that the most intense battles are waged. He writes, "Just as it is easier to sin by thought than by deed, so also is the war fought on the field of thought more severe than that which is conducted in the area of things and events. For the mind is easily moved indeed, and hard to control in the presence of sinful fantasies."

We repeat what St. Ephraim the Syrian wrote, "Just as it is natural for ocean rocks to be pounded by waves, similarly man will undoubtedly come into contact with assaults borne of thoughts."

Abba Zosima looked upon the battle we do in confronting and controlling *logismoi*, as that which gains us the crown of glory. He wrote:

> *St. Anthony used to say, "Take away the thoughts, and no one can become holy. One who avoids a beneficial temptation is avoiding eternal life." One of the saints said, "Who procured those crowns for the holy martyrs, except their persecutors? Who granted such great glory to Saint Stephen but they who stoned him? In addition, he always used to quote the passage from Evagrius: "I do not blame those who accuse me, but rather I call them my benefactors."*

Without the temptations that the *logismoi*, the thoughts, place in our path, no one can become holy; no one can gain the crown of glory. Thus, some of the Fathers looked upon *logismoi* as benefactors. It is in confronting and controlling thoughts that we receive the crown of glory.

THE ONASSIS FORMULA FOR WEALTH

Testifying to the power thoughts exert upon us, Aristotle Onassis once shared his formula for becoming a millionaire. He stated openly, "You have to think money day and night. You have to dream about money in your sleep as I do." Here is a perfect example of a person possessed by money, body, mind and soul.

When asked how he discovered the law of gravitation, Sir Isaac Newton replied, "By thinking about it all the time." Thoughts are powerful.

William Lyon Phelps said, "The belief that youth is the happiest time of life is a fallacy. The happiest person is the person who thinks the most interesting thoughts." And the most interesting thoughts are holy thoughts, pure thoughts, uplifting thoughts from God's Word.

IF YOU THINK YOU ARE BEATEN, YOU ARE

An unknown author wrote:

If you think you are beaten, you are;
If you think you dare not, you don't.
If you like to win, but think you can't
it's almost a cinch you won't.

If you think you'll lose, you've lost
for out in the world we find
success begins with a fellow's will;
it's all in the state of mind.

If you think you're outclassed, you are;
you've got to think high to rise,
you've got to be sure of yourself
before you can win the prize.

Life's battles don't always go
to the stronger or faster man;
but sooner or later the man who wins
is the man who thinks he can.

Thoughts are powerful. "The man who wins is the man who thinks he can."

The 1937 Nobel Prize winner in physiology and medicine, Dr. Albert Szent Gyorge, said, "Discovery consists of looking at the same thing as everyone else and thinking something different."

THROW YOUR MIND OVER THE BAR FIRST

You can change tomorrow by the thoughts you think today, for we form and shape our future by our thoughts. Faced with what he thought was an impossible task in an Olympic meet, a young contestant hesitated until the instructor came along, put his arm around the boy's shoulder and said, "Throw your mind over the bar first and your body will follow."

Disturbed when he saw tattooed on a person's body the three words, "Born to Lose," a person went to the Chinese tattoo artist and asked him how anyone would mark one's body with such a totally negative statement: "Born to Lose." The Chinese artist tapped his forehead and said, "Before tattoo on body, tattoo on mind."

Thoughts are powerful.

The Desert Fathers often used one thought to neutralize another thought. A younger brother asked an elder, "What shall I do? I am tortured by pride." The elder responded, "You are right to be proud. Was it not you who made heaven and earth?"

Another Desert Father said, "What condemns us is not that thoughts enter into us but that we use them badly; indeed, through our thoughts we can be shipwrecked, and through our thoughts we can be crowned."

"Keep your heart with all vigilance, from it flow the springs of life" (Prov. 4:23).

A TRANQUIL MIND IS HEALTH FOR THE BODY

A tranquil mind means health for the body. An untranquil mind leads to anxiety and depression. Satan delights in torturing us with anxious thoughts. He takes advantage of untranquil minds. *Logismoi,* thoughts, come to us both from God and from Satan. The Church Fathers tell us that the best way to discern whether the thoughts come from God or from Satan is to remember that the thoughts that come from God generate peace and joy, while *logismoi* that come from Satan cause anxiety and turmoil.

Mother Maria said once that she thought she had only one appearance of Christ in her life. It was when she was particularly depressed one day. Christ appeared to her and said, "Maria, take it easy. Relax. It ain't what you think." Thoughts that come from Satan cause much turmoil. Then Jesus comes and says, "Relax. It ain't what Satan made you think." Satan will almost always present the worst case scenario.

How much we need to heed the words of St. Paul:

> *Have no anxiety about anything, but in everything by prayer and supplication with thanksgiving let your requests be made known to God. And the peace of God, which passes all understanding, will keep your hearts and minds in Christ Jesus (Phil. 4:6-7).*

Pascal wrote:

> *Man is but a reed, the most feeble thing in nature; but he is a thinking reed.... All our dignity consists, then, in thought.... Let us endeavor, then, to think well.*

We honor God by thinking well. There are some people, however, who are too lazy even to think. One such person said once, "When I work, I works hard; when I sits, I sits loose; when I thinks, I fall asleep."

KILLED BY THIRTY YEARS OF THOUGHT

The following true story illustrates exactly how powerful thoughts are.

Killed by thirty years of thought.

> *So a London newspaper headlined its report of the strange death of a woman tennis star. This woman, as a small girl thirty years before, had watched in terror as her mother had died suddenly of a heart attack while being treated by a dentist. The traumatic experience so profoundly affected the child that in the thirty years that followed, she absolutely refused any dental treatment. The mere suggestion of going to a dentist terrified her. And this, despite the realization that the dentist to whom her mother had gone had no responsibility for her mother's death. It was merely a coincidence that the heart attack which caused her death occurred in a dentist's office.*
>
> *Finally, dental work became so necessary that the woman was compelled to have it done in spite of her terror. She insisted, however, that her physician accompany her to the dentist's office. But it was to no avail. As she sat in the dentist's chair, just like her mother had thirty years before, she was suddenly seized with a heart attack and died.*

Thirty years of thought had indeed killed her—thirty years of a killing fear thought. Consider how thirty years of faith thoughts, thirty years of enthusiastic thoughts, thirty years of positive, holy, Godly thoughts, might have changed the life of this woman.

"Keep your heart with all vigilance, for from it flow the springs of life" (Prov. 4:23). The writer of Proverbs might well have added "life and death." Both can issue from the heart.

"I LIVE IN MY MIND"

"I live in my mind," someone wrote. "I try to make it a sacred, holy and pleasant place to live in." St. Martyrius elaborated, "You should remember God at every moment, then your mind will become heaven."

St. Maximos explained how the mind can sin just as much as the body.

> *As the body is capable of fornication with the body of a woman, the mind can also fornicate with the thought of the woman, through the imagination of that same body. A man imagines in his mind the form of his own body to be united with the form of the woman's body. The same is true with the other sins as well. Those things which the body does actively in the physical world, the mind also does in the world of thoughts.*

Hence, the need for guarding the mind, vigilance, *nepsis*.

Sin is no mere skin disease; it is a mind-and-heart disease that threatens our destruction. Any sin committed by the body begins first in the mind, heart, and will of a person. Evil thoughts can only be put into practice by the body. The two work in collusion. That is why Isaac of Nineveh wrote:

> *Do not tempt your mind, for the sake of experience, by looking at base, seductive thoughts, while supposing that you are invincible. Even wise men have been troubled in this situation and gone wrong.*

Isaac believed that "the stairway to the kingdom of heaven is within you," in your mind and heart. The only way to ascend this stairway is through vigilance (*nepsis*), posting a guard at the door of the mind and heart.

Our modern world is greatly preoccupied with the exploration of outer space, and this is good. But we Christians should be even more preoccupied with the exploration of inner space, the mind and heart. Why? Because it is here that wars begin, and it is here that peace begins. It is here that hatred begins, and it is here that love begins. It is here that sin begins, and it is here that repentance begins. It is here that discouragement begins, and it is here that hope begins.

If our thoughts dwell in the gutter, we will live in the gutter. If our thoughts are directed toward the pure and noble things of life, we will walk the earth as children of God. Puny thoughts make puny people. Great thoughts make great people. Holy thoughts make holy people. "Above all else, keep your heart with all vigilance for from it flow the springs of life" (Prov. 4:23).

WHAT JESUS SAID ABOUT THOUGHTS

Jesus had much to say about thoughts. To the Pharisees, He said:

> *You wash the exterior of the cup and saucer, but inside you are full of licentiousness.... You are like white tombs, outside lovely, but inside full of bones of death and filth. Outside you appear just, but inside you are full of hypocrisy and wickedness" (Matt. 23:26-28).*

Commenting on these words of Jesus, St. Macarius the Great wrote:

> *What injures and corrupts a person is from within. Out of the heart proceed evil thoughts, as the Lord said (Mt. 15:19) since the things that corrupt a person are within. So, from within is the spirit of evil, creeping and progressing in the soul. It appears to reason. It incites. It is as the veil of darkness, the "old man" (2 Cor. 5:17) whom those who have recourse to*

God must put off, to don the heavenly and new man that is Christ (Eph. 4:22; col. 3:8). So nothing of the things that are outside can harm a person except the spirit of darkness that dwells in the heart, alive and active. Each person, then, in their thoughts, must engage in the struggle so that Christ may shine in the heart. To Him be glory for ever.

Macarius then goes on to describe the heart in apocalyptic terms:

The heart itself is but a small vessel, yet dragons are there, and there are also lions; there are poisonous beasts and all the treasures of evil. There are rough and uneven roads; there are precipices; but there too is God, the angels, life and the Kingdom, light and the apostles, the heavenly cities and treasures of grace. All things are within it.

Macarius moreover describes the heart in terms of an arena where life's great battles are to be fought.

To the Jews of His day who supposed that eating pork poisoned both soul and body, Jesus said:

Nothing that enters the mouth contaminates a man, but what comes out contaminates; because from the mind proceed bad thoughts, murders, adulteries, fornications, thefts, false testimonies, blasphemies. These are the things which defile a man" (Matt. 15:17-20).

And several times Jesus repeated the words, "A good man out of the good treasure of his heart brings forth good things; and an evil man out of the evil treasure brings forth evil things" (Matt. 12:35).

OUT OF THOUGHT GROWS SPEECH AND ACTION

Out of thought grows speech. Out of thought grows action. If I think wrongly, I will speak and act wrongly. If I think rightly, my speech and action will also be right. Thoughts are a mighty force; they are building my future; they are making my character. Fear thoughts, melancholy thoughts, lower vitality and cause depression. Whereas loving thoughts, peaceful thoughts, optimistic thoughts, Godly thoughts, strengthen and empower people. Therefore, writes St. Paul, "If there is anything that is pure, lovely, gracious, excellent, think on it."

And St. Paul writes in Romans 8:5-6:

> *For those who live according to the flesh set their minds on the things of the flesh, but those who live according to the Spirit, set their minds on the things of the Spirit. To set the mind on the flesh is death, but to set the mind on the Spirit is life and peace.*

St. John Cassian warns against entertaining thoughts of anger.

> *St. Paul said, "Do not let the sun go down upon your anger and do not make room for the devil," (Eph. 4:26-27) by which he means, "Do not make Christ, the Sun of Righteousness, set in your hearts by angering Him through your assent to evil thoughts, thereby allowing the devil to find room in you because of Christ's departure.... We must avoid anger not only in what we do but also in our thoughts; otherwise our intellect will be darkened by our rancour, cut off from the light of spiritual knowledge and discrimination, and be deprived of the indwelling of the Holy Spirit.*

WHENCE COME THE *LOGISMOI*?

What is the source of the *logismoi*?

St. Thalassios, one of the Fathers of the *Philokalia*, notes that:

> *There are three ways through which thoughts arise in you: through the senses, through the memory, and through the body's temperament. Of these the most irksome are those that come through the memory.*

Remembrance of wrongs can lead to bitter depression. Rehearsing the injustice done to them, refusing to be comforted prolongs the misery. One saint calls such remembrance of wrongs, "…the consummation of anger, hatred of righteousness, a worm of the mind, a nail stuck in the soul, continuous sin, unsleeping transgression, hourly malice."

St. John Chrysostom describes the remembrance of wrongs by comparing the situation to a man who walks by a house and is showered by a pail of filthy water dumped on him from an upper window. If this person goes back and walks there again every day, and continues to be drenched by buckets of filthy water, then one begins to wonder about what is wrong with him. So it is with the continual remembrance of wrongs. By perpetually remembering a wrong done to him once long ago, the person is making it happen again and again each and every day.

Such remembrance of wrongs keeps producing *logismoi* that poison the mind and heart. The antidote is forgiveness, repentance, and focusing on God's Word.

TO SET THE MIND ON THE FLESH IS DEATH

In view of these teachings on *logismoi*, what can we say to the misguided who believe that pornography, for example, has no ill effect on the mind?

Well, if bad literature has no evil influence on the mind, then logically good literature should also not have a healthy influence on people. Yet our whole system of education is based on the premise that through good literature the mind can be elevated and greatly benefited by noble ideas expressed in words, art and music.

We cannot have it both ways.

Some go even further and claim that pornography has therapeutic value, that it's actually good for us. If it is better to soak the mind with lust, to stain the soul with uncontrolled fantasy than to think about "whatever is pure, lovely, gracious," then life becomes a grotesque parody of everything we had thought it was supposed to mean. It becomes a "gutter" experience, rather than an experience of something noble.

St. Paul states it plainly, "To set the mind on the flesh is death, but to set the mind on the Spirit is life and peace." "Above all else, keep your heart with all vigilance, for from it flow the springs of life" (Prov. 4:23). "Let your thoughts be ever in the kingdom of heaven and soon you will possess it as a heritage" (Abba Hyperechius).

HAVE THE MIND OF CHRIST

St. Paul writes, "Let this mind be in you which was also in Christ Jesus" (Phil.2:5). What does it mean to have "the mind of Christ"? To have "the mind of Christ" is to have a mind of love. "I have loved you with an everlasting love," says the Lord. To have the mind of Christ is to love one's enemies and do good to them and pray for them. To have the mind of Christ is to go to the second mile. To have the mind of Christ is to have a mind of peace, "My peace I give to you, not as the world gives do I give to you," said Jesus. To have the mind of Christ is to have a mind of firmness in the hour of temptation and of calmness in the hour of death.

When do we receive "the mind of Christ"? When we are baptized, St. Paul tells us that we "put on Christ": "For as many of you as were baptized into Christ have put on Christ" (Gal. 3:27). It is at Baptism that we receive by God's grace "the mind of Christ."

Nikitas Stithatos, one of the *Philokalia* Fathers, explains how the mind of Christ operates in us:

> *Through the intellect, beholder of the light of divine life, we receive knowledge of God's hidden mysteries. Through the soul's faculty of judgment we winnow in the light of this knowledge the thoughts that arise within the heart, distinguishing the good from the bad. Through the discrimination of the intelligence we savour our conceptual images. Those that spring from a bitter root we transform into sweet nourishment for the soul, or else we reject them entirely; those that spring from a virtuous and vigorous stock we accept. In this way we take every thought captive and make it obey Christ (cf. 2 Cor. 10:5). Through the understanding of the intellect we smell the spiritual unguent of the grace of the Holy Spirit, our hearts filled with joy and gladness. Through the watchfulness of the heart we consciously perceive the Spirit, who refreshes the flame of our desire for supernal blessings and warms our spiritual powers, numbed as they have been by the frost of the passions.*

To have the mind of Christ is to have the mind of empathy, understanding, forgiveness, compassion, and kindness.

St. Maximus the Confessor describes the "mind of Christ" as follows:

> *According to the text, "But we have the mind of Christ" (1 Cor. 2:16), the saints are said to receive Christ's intellect. But this does not come to us through the loss of our own intellectual power; nor does it come to us as a supplementary part added to our intellect;*

nor does it pass essentially and hypostatically into our intellect. Rather, it illumines the power of our intellect with its own quality and conforms the activity of our intellect to its own. In my opinion, the person who has Christ's intellect is he whose thinking agrees with that of Christ and who apprehends Christ through all things.

"Do not be conformed to this world, but be transformed by the renewing of your mind, that you may prove what is the good and acceptable and perfect will of God" (Rom. 12:2). When the mind is renewed, it becomes the mind of Christ. It is an experience that renews and transfigures us.

THE MIND OF CHRIST YIELDS THE WISDOM OF GOD

To have the mind of Christ is to have the wisest teacher and the greatest mentor in the world. Jesus is smarter, more intelligent, than one trillion billion Einsteins put together. "In Him," writes St. Paul, "are hidden all the treasures of wisdom and knowledge" (Col. 2:3).

One writer described the mind and the wisdom of Christ as follows:

Our commitment to Jesus can stand on no other foundation than a recognition that He is the One who knows the truth about our lives and our universe.... He knew how to transform the tissues of the human body from sickness to health and from death to life. He knew how to suspend gravity, interrupt weather patterns, and eliminate unfruitful trees without saw or ax....

In the ethical domain He brought an understanding of life that has influenced world thought more than any other.... All these things show Jesus' cognitive and practical mastery of every phase of reality:

physical, moral, and spiritual....

He is not just nice, He is brilliant. He is the smartest man who ever lived. He is now supervising the entire course of world history (Rev. 1:5) while simultaneously preparing the rest of the universe for our future role in it (John 14:2). He always has the best information on everything and certainly also on the things that matter most in human life.

So, seek "the mind of Christ" and keep yourself plugged into His mind by reading and claiming His word day by day. "Let this mind be in you which was also in Christ Jesus" (Phil.2:5).

THINKING MAKES IT SO

I sometimes hear people repeating that old threadbare saying, "Thinking doesn't make it so." No greater error was ever voiced. Thinking does make it so! On this day you are what your thoughts have made you. You are what you have thought about for the past 10, 20, 30 or 40 years. And if you want to know what you will be ten years from now, the answer is simple. You will be what you're thinking about now, or what you will be thinking about during the next ten years.

Many of the Church Fathers talk about the sin of spiritual adultery. What is "spiritual adultery"? The fathers begin by reminding us that a Christian is married to Christ. When, instead of communing with Christ in one's mind, one chooses to have intercourse with the devil by welcoming evil thoughts, then one is committing what they call "spiritual adultery." This is what St. Paul calls "setting one's mind on the flesh," which leads to death.

St. Macarios of Egypt counsels that spiritual adultery is the consent one gives to evil thoughts. He writes:

A person is obliged to maintain his soul pure and clean, since it is the bride of Christ.

THE MIND IS A COMPUTER

Living as we do in the computer age, we are reminded in many ways how much our mind is like a computer. A person came home from work one evening looking haggard and lamenting, "We had a rough day, the computer broke down and we had to do all the thinking." The computer, of course, should not *replace* the mind but *extend* the work of the mind. The mind itself is like an internal computer that runs the whole person. It's a wonderful instrument. But just like a real computer, it has to be given the right program, if it's going to do its job well. It has to be programmed correctly. This applies to "the mind of Christ" that we received in Holy Baptism (Gal.3:27). The proper programming of "the mind of Christ" involves prayer and filling one's mind with thoughts that are "true, honest, just, pure, lovely and of good repute" (Phil. 4:8). It means memorizing and claiming passages of scripture such as:

> *Peace I leave with you, My peace I give unto you: not as the world gives, do I give to you. Let not your heart be troubled, neither let it be afraid (John 14:27).*
>
> *For God has not given us the spirit of fear, but of power, and of love, and of a sound mind (2 Tim. 1:7).*
>
> *Thou shalt keep him in perfect peace whose mind is stayed on Thee because he trusts in Thee (Is. 26:3).*

St. Theophan the Recluse wrote:

> *Every day keep turning over in your mind some thought which has deeply impressed you and fallen into your heart. Unless you exercise your powers of thought, the soul becomes numb.*

The mind is like a clock that is constantly running down,

someone said. It has to be wound up daily with good thoughts.

We need to start storing God's powerful words in our memory bank as well as in our heart.

A friend who came down with a serious illness and was confined for a long time said to me that what really sustained him during that stressful period were the promises from God's word which he had memorized and kept repeating and claiming each day. Truly, as our Lord said, "Man does not live by bread alone, but by every word that proceeds from the mouth of God."

A disciple said to his elder one day,"Master, I have gone thoroughly through Scripture. What more do I lack?" The elder answered, "Dear Child, the question is not, Have you gone through Scripture? The question is, has scripture gone through you?"

When we allow God's word to go "through us," it has a purifying, life-changing, sustaining, vivifying and uplifting effect upon us. We read in Luke 2:19, "But Mary kept all these things, pondering them in her heart." She feasted her mind and heart on the marvelous promises of God. She kept the promises and the promises kept her.

Above all else, keep your heart with all vigilance, for from it flow the springs of life (Prov. 4:23).

"GARBAGE IN - GARBAGE OUT"

Persons who work with computers have a saying that has become quite popular: "Garbage in - garbage out." What they mean is that you cannot get anything more out of a computer than what you put in. If poor data are fed into a computer, a poor printout is what you will receive. The things we put into our minds influence what comes out. Some people wonder why they have trouble with evil thoughts. And yet they watch television with no thought given to the quality of what is entering their minds. But there it is! "Garbage in - garbage out."

Others have problems because of the negative tapes about

themselves and others that they keep playing over and over in their minds. They need to turn off those negative tapes and turn on some positive ones. How? By doing what St. Paul suggests in Phil. 4:8:

> *Finally brethren, whatever is true, whatever is honorable, whatever is right, whatever is pure, whatever is lovely, whatever is of good repute, if there is any excellence and if there is anything worthy of praise, let your mind dwell on these things.*

Right here, in 40 clear words, St. Paul gives us the recipe for the kind of thoughts we should be feeding our minds. Paul knew that the human mind will always be dwelling on something. We are what we think, and Paul says we should discipline ourselves to think on things that are "true, honest, honorable, pure, of good repute, excellent and worthy of praise."

Sadly, it is part of our secular mindset today that if a serial killer commits a series of grisly murders, someone will write a book about him which will eventually become a movie. But instead of looking inside the mind of a maniacal serial killer to discover the dark thoughts that made him kill, how much more edifying it would be to look inside the mind of a saintly and virtuous person to lay bare the pure, holy, and noble thoughts that produced goodness and nobility in his life.

Why doesn't this happen? Because we live in a fallen world. But it can happen if we nurture our mind and feed on God's word daily.

WHAT DO YOU THINK OF YOURSELF?

Of all the aspects of thinking, one of the most important is: What do we think of ourselves? Ultimately, we become like that which we think we are. We become what our self-image tells us we are. If you think of yourself as defeated, that is what you will be.

What you *think*, you *are*.

Your self image determines what you will become. If you see yourself as a child of God, you will become and act like a child of God.

How does one acquire a healthy self image? First, we need to remember that one of the great destroyers of a healthy self-image is sin. After one sins, the self-image suffers terribly. One begins to be tortured with feelings of unworthiness. One begins to hate oneself. This is why it is so important to come to Christ with our sins every day, to repent, and seek forgiveness. Only the forgiveness of Christ can give us a self we can live with.

How else can we change our thinking about ourselves, our self image? Mainly by focusing on what God thinks of us. When asked, "What do you think of yourself?", the Christian will reply, "I think of myself as a child of God, loved by Him, redeemed by His precious blood, destined to live with Him to all eternity. Because of this, I will love myself. I will not act as a worthless nobody, but as a precious somebody, the child of a king. I will not allow sin to make me feel worthless because there is no sin that our Lord will not forgive once we repent. I will not allow failure to make me feel inferior, for, with God's help, failure can become a stepping stone to something higher and better. Even if people look down on me, I shall remember that God does not; He loves me with an everlasting love. And this is what counts."

I shall endeavor to love myself always as an important person, deeply loved by God. And I will try to love others that they too may come to love themselves as children of God and live up to the image God has of them. "As a man thinks in his heart, so is he," applies in a very special way to the image we have of ourselves.

HOW SHOULD I THINK OF MYSELF?

The Bible teaches that we should not think too highly of ourselves. But it makes it equally clear that we should not demean ourselves either. If the devil comes to you and whispers that you are no good, don't argue with him. In fact, you may as well admit it, but then remind him: "Regardless of what you say about me, I must tell you how the Lord feels about me. He tells me that I am so precious to Him that He gave Himself for me on the Cross! Will you call worthless—will you call a nobody—one for whom the Son of God died?"

In view of this, it is obvious that love of self is totally proper. If God loves us, we must love ourselves. There is a proper love of self as well as an improper love of self. We must love ourselves with the proper love with which God loves us. This flows from who we are in Christ.

There is a beautiful story entitled the *Fourth Temptation of Jesus*. It goes like this. Wracked by grinding pain and despair, Jesus looks down from the Cross and sees that even His disciples have forsaken Him. He sees the soldiers at the foot of the Cross gambling and laughing. He hears the taunts of spectators nearby. In that emotion-filled moment Satan whispers the fourth and final temptation into our Savior's ear, "They are not worth it. Face it, Jesus. They are just not worth it!" It was at that moment that Jesus raised His voice and said, "Father, forgive them, for they know not what they do." Jesus placed an expensive price tag on us when He died for us.

A CRITIQUE ON "THE POWER OF POSITIVE THINKING"

There is a typically American school of thought that has grown up around the subject of the power of thinking. It is called "the power of positive thinking." It was a Christian minister, Norman Vincent Peale, who coined the term and wrote a best-selling book on the subject. Many Christians consider the positive thinking philosophy to be part of their Christian faith. But when one examines Norman Vincent Peale's theology, one discovers that it is not totally consonant with the historic Christian faith. Dr. William Kilpatrick, a noted psychologist, who has critiqued Norman Vincent Peale, writes this about

Peale's theology, "It is faith in self rather than faith in God."

Norman Vincent Peale's philosophy, for example, comes perilously close to a faith in the sheer power of believing. The object of faith (God) seems almost secondary. Although Peale wants us to believe in God, he seems primarily concerned with belief as a psychological mechanism for achieving successful living. And he puts an extraordinary emphasis on believing in ourselves. *

Charles Fillmore of the Unity School of Christianity is another example of this positive thinking school of thought. He writes:

> *You can do everything with the thoughts of your mind. They are under your absolute control. You can direct them. You can coerce them. You can hush them or crush them. You can dissolve them and put others in their place. There is no other spot in the universe where man has mastery. The dominion that is yours by divine right is over your own thoughts. When man apprehends this and commences to exercise that dominion, he has begun to open the way to God, the only door to God – through mind and thought.*

Yet when one looks at the Bible and the stories of the saints throughout history, one fails to find such success through positive thinking. One fails to find saints offering personal testimonies on how they overcame anger, or greed, or any kind of mental temptation. On the contrary, one finds great emphasis on constant, unremitting *ascesis* and struggle to the very end of life with what the Church Fathers call *logismoi* or thoughts. The battle against *logismoi* is an on-going battle of falling and rising until at the end we rise more than fall, and that only by God's grace.

**Psychological Seduction*, Wm. Kilpatrick, Thomas Nelson Publ. Nashville, TN, 1983.

LOGISMOI OR THOUGHTS: GOOD AND BAD

As we have seen, the Fathers of the *Philokalia* and the spirituality they developed have much to say on the subject of thoughts or *logismoi*. Thoughts are not all bad; there are good thoughts. They show that we have a mind that is functioning well. Plato said, "Thinking is the talking of the soul to itself." Not all thoughts are evil. If an evil thought is the seed of sin, one needs to remember that the origin of the virtues is also to be found in thoughts—good thoughts. In fact, the voice of conscience is also part of the *nous* (mind). In order to distinguish between them, Origen called the good thought *logismos katharos*, a clean thought, and the impure thought, *logismos akatharos*, an unclean thought.

When the spiritual writers of the *Philokalia* use the word *logismos*, as we have pointed out, they refer mostly to evil thoughts, the kind of thoughts we ought not to have. The Fathers of the *Philokalia* describe *logismoi* as essentially a train of thoughts that befog and pollute the mind so that bit by bit it drifts away from reality into a world of fantasy. The Desert Fathers also teach that thoughts are caused by demons. Such thoughts are the seeds of the passions, those impulses that emerge from the unconscious and soon become obsessive.

Logismoi are important because all battles are won or lost first in the internal dialogue of the mind. For example, virtue is natural to us, while vice is unnatural. Yet vice is made to appear far more attractive than virtue because the *logismoi* step in, and backed by demons, darken the mind, preventing it from seeing the beauty of virtue, while clothing vice with an artificial attractiveness.

THE INVISIBLE STRUGGLE

John Cassian uses the image of a battlefield to describe the mind and heart where the demons attack us. St. Gregory of Sinai writes of fighting for Christ "in the stadium" or the "arena of the mind" wherein the devil tries "to force us to sacrifice our mind to the idol of sensuousness." Elias the Presbyter writes in the *Philokalia,* "You will not be able to cut down the passions raging within you unless you first leave untilled the soil from which they are fed, i.e., the mind." Pseudo-Macarius writes, "A man's whole effort should be employed upon his thoughts. He must cut away the brush of evil thoughts which besets him." Origen wrote, "The spring and source of every sin are evil thoughts. This is the invisible struggle."

Repeating what one Desert Father said:

> *It is not because evil thoughts come to us that we are condemned, but only because we make use of the evil thoughts. It can happen that from these thoughts we suffer shipwreck, but it can also happen that because of them we may be crowned.*

One Church Father calls on us to imitate the bee and not the fly. The bee goes from one flower to another while the fly is attracted to dung, he says.

CONTAMINATION OF THE SOUL

When we allow *logismoi,* evil thoughts, to enter the heart, they contaminate the heart like viruses. When negative *logismoi* enter the bloodstream, they have the same effect as a needle full of poison. The poison penetrates and spreads the deadly substance through the entire psyche. The heart is then contaminated to the point of death. To counteract such contamination, we need to create spiritual antibodies to destroy the deadly viruses of the *logismoi.* Such spiritual antibodies are created through vigilance, repentance, the Sacrament of Penance, the reading of God's Word, the Eucharist, and the Jesus Prayer. Some Church Fathers say that after our minds are purified and unified through the Jesus Prayer, "our thoughts swim like happy dolphins in a calmed sea."

THE PROCESS OF SIN THROUGH THE MIND

The Church Fathers, who spent their lives resisting the devil's onslaughts (*logismoi*) have a deep understanding of how Satan attacks us through the mind. They list the following four stages of how Satan attacks us through *logismoi*:

1. The mind receives a suggestion or stimulation, which is another word for temptation. This is called *prosbole* in Greek. It is like Satan knocking on the door. If the mind is vigilant, attentive, it will notice the provocation and will close the door on temptation, or, as some Church Fathers say, "If the devil knocks on the door of your mind, send Jesus to the door." By this they mean the Jesus Prayer. There is no sin involved in this first stage. Even Jesus was tempted.
2. If we do not close the door, the soul will enter into dialogue with the suggestion/temptation as Eve did with the serpent. The Fathers warn us about the great danger of dialoguing with Satan, since he is far wiser than we are with countless years of experience in seducing victims. This second step is called *syndiasmos* or dialogue. Yet even in this second stage of temptation there is no accountability, since no sin has been committed. It is a conversation, albeit dangerous, between Satan and the soul.
3. There is a union or coupling with the thought in which the mind consents to the temptation (*logismos*) and begins to dwell on it. The decision has been made. This is called *synkatathesis*, or consent. It is the beginning of sin. It is the stage Jesus referred to when He said that if you look upon a woman lustfully and covet her in your heart, it is as if you have already committed adultery.

Yet we are still in the third stage of consent. No action has taken place. It is still possible by God's grace to be liberated from this stage of consent.

During the fifth century certain very austere Christian zealots insisted that to consent to a *logismos* is the same as if one had already committed the sin. To convince these zealots that there was still a distance between consenting to a sin in one's heart and actually committing it, St. John Chrysostom invited them to a gourmet dinner. He instructed the cooks to prepare the most tempting dishes. He notified his guests not to eat during the day so as to be able to enjoy all the delicious food at the dinner. The guests arrived with a ravenous appetite. The servants began loading the table with sumptuous dishes. Before the meal, Chrysostom invited his deacon to read from the Psalms. The deacon read and kept on reading, twenty, thirty, forty minutes, with no end in sight. The guests agonized. They wondered if they would ever begin to eat. They were salivating with an overpowering desire to eat. Finally the prayer concluded. Then, Chrysostom turned and told his guests, "Now you may leave for home." They were shocked. "Why do you look so puzzled?" he asked them. "Didn't you see the food? Didn't you covet the food with great desire?" "Yes," they replied. "Well, then, it was as if you ate the food," said Chrysostom. Through this practical joke, the great saint was able to convince these austere zealots that there is a difference between consenting to sin in one's heart and actually committing it. It is still possible, even in the late state of consent, not to proceed to the last stage, from which a person can no longer retreat.

4. The fourth and last stage in the process of sin is the stage of captivity. Here we fall so completely under the power of the temptation that we are no longer free to resist it. It becomes a passion, an obsession, an addiction. We become its captive. We are imprisoned by it.

St. Hesychios describes this process of temptation as follows in the *Philokalia:*

> *The provocation comes first, then our coupling with it, or the mingling of our thoughts with those of the wicked demons. Third comes our assent to the provocation, with both sets of intermingling thoughts contriving how to commit the sin in practice. Fourth comes the concrete action – that is, the sin itself. If, however, the intellect is attentive and watchful, and at once repulses the provocation by counter-attacking and gainsaying it and invoking the Lord Jesus, its consequences remain inoperative; for the devil, being a bodiless intellect, can deceive our souls only by means of fantasies and thoughts. David was speaking about these provocations of the devil when he said: "Early in the morning I destroyed all the wicked of the earth, that I might cut off all evildoers from the city of the Lord" (Ps. 101:8. LXX); and Moses was referring to the act of assent to a provocation in his words: "You shall make no covenant with them, nor with their gods" (Exod. 23:32).*
>
> *Intellect is invisibly interlocked in battle with intellect, the demonic intellect with our own. So from the depths of our heart we must at each instant call on Christ to drive the demonic intellect away from us and in His compassion give us the victory.*

Tito Colliander describes the process as follows:

> *The impulse knocks like a salesman at the door. If one lets him in, he begins his sales talk about his wares, and it is hard to get rid of him even if one observes that his wares are not good. Thus follows consent and finally the purchase, often against one's own will.**

It all begins with the initial "knock" on the door.

1. a suggestion *(prosbole);*
2. a dialogue *(syndiasmos);*
3. consent *(synkatathesis);*
4. captivity, passion, or obsession.

A CAGED ENEMY

Demons who work through *logismoi* have freedom only to the extent that we allow them to have influence over us. They have no authority to do whatever they wish. They cannot enter where they are not wanted or invited. "Christ is Risen and the demons have fallen," wrote St. Chrysostom. The demons have been defeated by Jesus and placed in a cage like a lion or a tiger. But we have the freedom to walk up to the cage, unlock the gate, and let the tiger (*logismos*) out. This happens when we open the door to the *logismos* through *syndiasmos* (dialogue) and *synkatathesis* (consent).

HOW TO RESIST THE *LOGISMOI*

How can we best resist the *logismoi* or evil thoughts that attack us? Every day we need to make a decision as to which thoughts we will allow to enter our minds. We need to screen them carefully and with great discernment: What we read; what we watch on TV; what movie we see; what company we keep.

**The Way of Ascetics,* Tito Colliander. SVS Press. Crestwood, NY, 1960.

We need to "take every thought captive to Christ" (2 Cor. 10:5). The mind of Christ can, through the Holy Spirit, control our thoughts, our intents, and our actions, if we submit to Him daily.

A little girl, after a wonderful day of play, said to her mother at bedtime, "I have had such a happy time today." "I am glad," said the mother, "but tell me what made this day any different from yesterday?" After a short pause, the little girl replied, "Well, yesterday, I let my thoughts push me around, but today I pushed my thoughts around."

Jesus gives us the power to "push our thoughts around," to control them, to keep them from victimizing and enslaving us.

VICTORY CAN BE OURS

We can be assured of victory in our battle against *logismoi*, evil thoughts, for one very important reason. We have God's help whereas the devil does not and cannot ever have God's help. As Father Matta El-Maskeen wrote:

> *The mind of man...has the advantage over its enemy in one most important aspect: namely ... the devil has been completely and eternally forbidden any divine help. But man, on the other hand, has been from the very beginning God's beloved who was never once deprived of the all-powerful divine mercy.*

Because God's help is ever just a prayer away from us, St. Philotheos of Sinai was able to say:

> *Be extremely strict in guarding your intellect. When you perceive an evil thought, rebut it and immediately call upon Christ to defind you; and while you are still speaking, Jesus in His gentle love will say: "Behold, I am by your side ready to help you."*

Because of the help we receive from Christ, we can interpret the psalm of the exiles that recommends the dashing of the "children of Babylon" against the rocks, as the Desert Fathers interpreted it. For them, the "children of Babylon" symbolized evil thoughts, *logismoi*. The rock against which they are dashed was none other than Christ. For us today, the Jesus Prayer becomes the rock against which the evil thoughts are dashed.

THE NETS ON THE WINDOWS OF THE TEMPLE OF SOLOMON

St. Nicodemus of the Holy Mountain uses a powerful illustration from the Temple of Solomon to help us control sinful thoughts. He writes:

> *The windows of the Temple of Solomon were covered with fine nets to prevent the entry of impure insects (cf. Ez. 41:6). This may serve as a reminder that he who does not want any impure passions of the senses to enter into his soul must drape his senses with [spiritual] nets. What are these nets? It is the memory of death, for one; our account before Christ on the day of judgment; the memory of eternal suffering. Through these, man can put away the evil passions and sins, when they come before his eyes and his other senses. St. Neilos has confirmed that this is so: "Those who desire to keep their mind as a clean and pure temple, where the doors and windows are covered with fine nets to prevent the entry of any impure insects, must similarly cover their senses by meditating on the sobering realities of the future judgment which prevent any impure images from creeping in.*

A SPIRITUAL FILTERING SYSTEM

Recently a friend filled his pool with city water. It was murky green. "You mean I drink that water?" a friend asked. "Yes," he was told. He continued, "As purifying chemicals are added to the water, it becomes crystal clear. And the filtering system keeps it that way." It made me think of the spiritual filtering system that the Fathers of the *Philokalia* have given us to help filter and purify the thoughts that enter our mind. Evagrios the solitary describes this spiritual filtering system when he writes:

> *Call to mind what is even now going on in hell. Think of the suffering, the bitter silence, the terrible moaning, the great fear and agony, the dread of what is to come, the unceasing pain, the endless weeping. Remember, too, the day of your resurrection and how you will stand before God. Imagine that fearful and awesome judgment seat. Picture all that awaits those who sin: their shame before God the Father and His Anointed, before angels, archangels, principalities and all mankind. Think of all the forms of punishment: the eternal fire, the worm that does not die, the abyss of darkness, the gnashing of teeth, the terror and the torments. Then picture all the blessings that await the righteous: Intimate communion with God the Father and His Anointed, with angels, archangels, principalities and all the saints, the kingdom and its gifts, the gladness and the joy. Picture (all) these states. This will help you to escape thoughts that are defiling and harmful.*

So, keep the windows to the five senses covered with the spiritual nets of prayer and vigilance (*nepsis*). Meditate regularly on the fearful and awesome judgment; think of heaven and hell. Let these become some of the spiritual nets and filters through which to sift all thoughts, *logismoi*, that seek to enter the mind and heart.

A brother once asked a certain Elder:

> *What shall I do when filthy thoughts are killing my soul? The old man replied: When a mother wants to wean her child, she applies a bitter herb to her breast, and when the baby comes as usual to suckle and tastes it, it moves away because of the bitterness it has tasted. You must also use something bitter. What does this mean, father? Instead of a herb, bring to your mind the remembrance of death and the punishments of the next life. Many ascetics kept in their cell a skull which helped them in their uninterrupted remembrance of death, which in turn gathers the* nous *and makes the heart contrite.*

MORE SPIRITUAL FILTERS

St. Theodoros, the Great Ascetic, another one of the *Philokalia* Fathers, mentions this same spiritual filtering system through which we should sift the thoughts that come to us. He writes:

> *Bring to mind the punishment that befalls sinners, the reproach, the reprobation of the conscience, how they will be rejected by God and cast into the agelong fire.... Meditate on all the other chastisements, and let your tears continually drench your cheeks...*
>
> *I have known many people in whom such thoughts have produced an abundance of tears, and who in this way have wonderfully cleansed all the powers of their soul. But think also of the blessings which await the righteous: How they will stand at Christ's right hand, the gracious voice of the Master, the inheritance of the heavenly kingdom,... the sweet light, the endless joy, never interrupted by grief, those heavenly mansions, life with the angels, and all the other promises*

made to those who fear the Lord. Let these thoughts dwell with you, sleep with you, arise with you. See that you never forget them but, wherever you are, keep them in mind, so that evil thoughts may depart and you may be filled with divine solace.

SELAH

An odd little word is used in the Psalms. It is always found at the end of a sentence. It's like an exclamation point, emphasizing a truth that was presented. It's the word *Selah,* and it means, "Stop! Think! Meditate on what you just read!" This is the word the Fathers of the *Philokalia* ask us to use when we are assaulted by evil thoughts. Stop. Think. Pay attention. *Proscomen* in Greek. Pay attention. Be vigilant. Meditate on the thought that you will one day die. You will appear before God. You will have to answer to Him for every evil thought you invited and entertained in your mind. *Selah.*

"Stop! Focus, think, concentrate, meditate," writes William A. Ward:

not on the problem, but on the peace;
not on the conflict, but on the Comforter;
not on the difficulty, but on the door;
not on the crisis, but on the Christ;
not on the worry, but on the way;
not on the imperfect, but on the infinite;
not on the trouble, but on the Truth;
not on the scarcity, but on the supply;
not on the dilemma, but on the Deliverer;
not on the mistake, but on the Master;
not on the pain, but on the Physician;
not on the worst, but on the Word;
not on the glum, but on the Guide;
not on the sorrow, but on the Spirit;
not on the obstacle, but on the Omnipotent.

POST A GUARD AT THE GATE

In addition to passing each thought through the spiritual filter of having to stand before Christ one day and having to answer to Him for the thoughts we welcomed into our mind, the Church Fathers suggest other ways to control thoughts.

They advise us to post a guard at the gate of the mind and to be the doorkeeper of our heart.

St. Theophan the Recluse wrote:

> *After every thought has been banished from the soul by the memory of God's presence, stand at the door of the heart and watch carefully everything that enters or goes out from there.*

St. Nicodemos of the Holy Mountain issues a clarion call to guard all the senses which he calls gateways to sin:

> *St. Isaac has noted, the enemy is standing and observing day and night directly against our eyes to detect which entrance of our senses will be opened for him to enter. Once he enters through one of our senses because of our lack of vigilance, then this devious shameless dog attacks us further with his own arrows. We must also struggle to protect our senses because it is not only through curious eyes that we fall into the sin of desire and commit fornication and the adultery of the heart, as the Lord noted. There is also the fornication and the adultery of the sense of hearing, the sense of smell, the sense of taste, the sense of touch, and all of the senses together. Therefore, St. Gregory the Theologian has written in his heroic counsel to the virgin: "Virgin, be truly a virgin in the ears, in the eyes and in the tongue! Every sense that wanders with ease, sins." St. Gregory of Nyssa also said, "The Lord has spoken, I believe, about all the senses, so that following*

His words we can conclude that the one who hears lustfully, the one who touches and the one who uses every inner power in us (lustfully) to serve pleasure has actually committed them in his heart."

GUARD THE SENSES

The wise St. Syncletike said:

Even when we do not want it, the thieves will enter through the senses. For how is it possible for a house not to be darkened by the smoke entering from outside through the doors and windows that have been left opened?

Evagrius of Pontus warns:

Be the door-keeper of your heart and do not let any thought come in without questioning it. Question each thought individually: "Are you on our side or the side of our foes?" And if it is one of ours, it will fill you with tranquility.

The *Philokalia* calls on us to be vigilant:

Vigilance is a firm control of the mind. Post it at the door of the heart, so that it sees marauding thoughts as they come, hears what they say, and knows what these robbers are doing, and what images are being projected…so as to seduce the mind by fantasy.

The ever-vigilant guard who is posted at the gate must keep throwing out what the devil throws in, as the following story of the early fathers illustrates:

An old man said to a brother, "The devil is the

enemy and you yourself are the house. The enemy never stops throwing all that he finds into your house, pouring all sorts of impurities over it. It is your part not to neglect throwing them outside again. If you do not do this the house will be filled with all sorts of impurities and you will no longer be able to get inside. But all that the other begins to throw in, you should throw out again little by little, and by the grace of Christ your house will remain pure."

St. Casian explains why posting a guard at the gate of the mind is essential. He writes:

While the children of Babylon – by which I mean our wicked thoughts – are still young, we should dash them to the ground and crush them against the rock, which is Christ (Ps. 137:0; 1 Cor. 10:4). If these thoughts grow stronger because we assent to them, we will not be able to overcome them without much pain and labor.

DON'T BUILD AN AIRPORT

Thoughts, like airplanes, fly over us, but we don't have to build an airport for them to land. Post a guard at the gate, using the spiritual radar of watchfulness (*nepsis*) and prayer. Both watchfulness and prayer serve as an early warning system against Satan's attacks. St. Philotheos of Sinai writes:

From dawn we should stand bravely and unflinchingly at the gate of the heart, with true remembrance of God and unceasing prayer of Jesus Christ in the soul; and keeping watch with the intellect, we should slaughter all the sinners of the land (cf. Ps. 101:8 LXX). Given over in the intensity of our ecstasy to the constant remembrance of God, we should for the

> *Lord's sake cut off the heads of the tyrants (cf. Hab. 3:14. LXX), that is to say, we should destroy hostile thoughts at their first appearance.*

Hesychius of Jerusalem says that we can be free of sin by guarding the mind. "If you have some great treasure in your house, you stand guard at the door," he says. The treasure, of course, is the image of God in us. St. Anthony observes, "The mind, loved by God, has a watchful gatekeeper, who closes its doors to evil and base thoughts." If someone were to come into your home with a pail of garbage with the intent of dumping it on your living room floor, would you not offer resistance? How much more ought we to resist those who seek to dump garbage into the living temple of God's presence: our soul.

ANCIENT EGYPT

In ancient Egypt the Pharaohs were often portrayed with a cobra poised over their heads. King Tut is pictured not only with headgear featuring a cobra—but also with a vulture. The cobra was to attack the poisonous thoughts before they entered his mind. The vulture was there to consume them. Fortified by prayer, watchfulness, the Eucharist, and the Holy Spirit, God enables us to become powerful gatekeepers of the mind, warding off the *logismoi*, the evil thoughts that eventually become the seeds of passions.

Foremost among the weapons of resistance to evil thoughts, according to the spirituality of the *Philokalia*, is the Jesus Prayer. As we read in the *Philokalia*:

> *It is impossible to purify our heart from passion-filled thoughts and to get rid of the demons from the heart without the unceasing invocation of the name of Jesus Christ.*

"Lord Jesus, Son of God, have mercy on me, the sinner."

CLOSE THE DOOR!

Is it possible ever to be free of *logismoi*, evil thoughts? According to Origen, it is impossible to be entirely free of evil thoughts. They will keep knocking on the door of our mind, but we can keep closing the door on them. When they knock, we can keep sending Jesus to the door through the Jesus Prayer. It is important not to dwell upon them and converse with them, as Eve did. St. Maximus the Confessor wrote:

> *The Bible does not forbid us from thinking on some things – they were meant to be thought of – only avoid dwelling on them with immoderate eagerness.*

We must not allow them to enter the paradise of the heart. A thought does not become sinful unless one opens the door to it, welcomes it into the living room of the soul and then acts upon it.

One of the Desert Fathers tells the following story:

> *A brother said to an elder, "I see no warfare in my heart." The old man said to him, "You are a building open on all sides, and whoever wishes can pass through you and you are unaware of it. If you have a door, you should shut it, and not allow wicked thoughts to enter through it; for then you will see them standing outside and attacking you."*

If someone comes to your door and knocks and there is no answer, in all probability, that person will knock again. If it is someone who is persistent, he may knock on the window, or perhaps go around to the back door. And if there is still no reply, he will leave. It is the same with fears, worries and negative thoughts of any kind. If they find no response, they will leave. That is why it is so important to keep the door of the soul closed to *logismoi*.

St. Silouan the Athonite had this advice for those who battle intrusive thoughts:

> *The saints learned how to do battle with the enemy. They knew that the enemy uses intrusive thoughts to deceive us, and so all through their lives they declined such thoughts. At first sight there seems to be nothing wrong about an intrusive thought but soon it begins to divert the mind from prayer, and then stirs up confusion. The rejection of all intrusive thoughts, however apparently good, is therefore essential, and equally essential is it to have a mind pure in God.... But should an intrusive thought approach, there is no cause to be troubled. Put your trust in God and continue in prayer. We must not be troubled, because that rejoices the enemy. Pray, and the intrusive thought will leave you. This is the way of the saints.**

LEARN TO SAY NO

St. Poimen the Ascetic (5th century) tells the following story about resisting *logismoi*:

> *A brother came to Abba Poimen and said, "Many distracting thoughts come into my mind, and I am in danger because of them." Then the elder thrust him out into the open air and said, "Open up the garments about your chest and catch the wind in them." But he replied, "This I cannot do." So the elder said to him, "If you cannot catch the wind, neither can you prevent distracting thoughts from coming into your head. Your job is to say 'NO' to them."*

**St. Silouan the Athonite,* Archimandrite Sophrony. Stavropegic Monastery of St. John the Baptist. Essex, England. 1991.

There are several ways of saying no to *logismoi*. One person responds by saying, "I am very sorry; I am here, but not for you." By saying no to unwelcome thoughts, we close the door on them. We purposefully reject them and refuse to entertain them. We say to them firmly, "Get out. You are a troublemaker. You are not welcome here. I never want to see you or hear from you again." They will obey if you are persistent enough. No person wants to stay where he is not wanted. In the past, negative thoughts may have been your companions only because you have invited, enjoyed and cherished them. Or you may have given them space because you were ignorant of the harm they could do.

But now it's different. Now, by God's grace, you can say "no" to them. You can refuse to open the door when they knock. God designed the stomach to eject what is bad for it through vomiting. Not so with the human brain. He has left that up to us. He has given us free will and His grace to reject them. In rejecting sinful thoughts, one word is often more effective than a dozen words, so when you find yourself encountering a demonic thought of any kind, simply invoke the all-powerful name of Jesus either audibly or silently. In other words, when the devil knocks, send Jesus to the door. One of the Desert Fathers, John the Dwarf, who practiced this, wrote:

> *I sit in my cell and I am aware of evil thoughts coming against me, and when I have no more strength against them, I take refuge in God by prayer and I am saved from the enemy.*

THE IMPORTANCE OF SAYING "NO"

We reject evil thoughts by saying no to them. The first thing we do upon becoming a Christian in Holy Baptism is to say "No". The priest calls on us to say no, to reject the evil one and all of his works, "Do you renounce Satan, and all of his angels, and all of his works, and all of his services, and all his pride?"

The same question is asked *three* times! Then the priest asks a similar question *three* more times. "Have you renounced Satan?" Then he says to the one being baptized, "Breathe and spit upon him!" Then as we turn to face Christ (East), he calls on us to say "Yes" to Christ and to bow down before Him.

Fr. Alexander Schmemann explained the meaning of this renunciation of the devil in Baptism when he wrote, "the first act of the Christian life is a renunciation, a challenge. No one can be Christ's until he has first faced evil to acknowledge its reality, to know its power, and to proclaim the power of God to destroy it. The exorcisms announce the forthcoming Baptism as an act of victory."*

A LIFE-LONG "NO" TO EVIL

It is significant that the Christian life begins with a call to renounce the devil, to say no to him. One cannot be a follower of Jesus, one cannot receive the new life of Christ in Holy Baptism unless one is willing to say —and to keep saying throughout one's life—"no" to the temptations of the evil one. The act of renouncing the devil in Baptism sets the tone for the life of the Christian: it will be a life of struggle and spiritual conflict with the devil until the day we die. Thus, renouncing the devil emphasizes the negative aspect of Baptism: death to sin and the lifelong struggle against it.

THE POWERFUL LITTLE WORD "NO"

Thus, the Christian life begins with a "no." A distinguished writer once asked, "In your opinion, what word in the English language is the most useful?" After thinking a moment the writer replied, "The word no." Pythagoras said, "The oldest short words—Yes and No—are those which require most thought." Part of the ability to grow up and be your own person

**For the Life of the World.* A. Schmemann. National Student Christian Federation. New York, 1963.

is to learn to say no to what others want you to be and to say yes to what God has called you to be.

When one mother asked her college freshman daughter about sex pressures on campus, the daughter answered, "I'm into women's lib, and I'm learning to be my own person. That includes the right to say no!"

When Pilate failed to say no, a just man was turned over to an angry mob to be crucified (Matt. 27:22-29).

One parent wrote, "No is the greatest gift of love I can give my child. Ultimately my 'no' allows the child to say 'no' to himself, and to others and to Satan."

The word "no" served as Christ's barricade against the tempter (Matt. 4:3-11) and it serves as our barricade against temptation today.

The little word *no* is of more importance than almost any other word in our vocabulary. It is saying *no* to Jesus that leads a person to hell; it is that little but powerful word *no* directed to Satan that preserves chastity, morality, and sanity in our insane world. It is the lack of that little *no* in many cases that leads us into all kinds of trouble.

A super-powerful car with no brakes is not super-powerful. It is weak. In fact, it is dangerous. Brakes are all-important in a car. So is the ability to say *no*.

In order to say *yes* to pure love, I must learn to say *no* to impure love or lust. In order to say *yes* to my dear spouse, I must keep saying *no* to unfaithfulness, adultery. In order to say *yes* to God's beautiful gift of sex, I must keep saying *no* when Satan tempts me with thoughts of lust (*logismoi*).

A mother asked her daughter one day, "Do you know what the most effective oral contraceptive is?" "No," said the daughter. "You said it," replied the mother. It's that tiny but powerful word *no*.

A former governor was asked, "What is the hardest task a governor has?" He answered simply, "Saying no." And saying *no* is often the small end of what may become an unmanageable problem.

What is the source of happiness? It is self-control, self-mastery, the ability to take hold of yourself and say *no* to that which is wrong. That is what takes and makes muscle. That is what makes people strong and happy. That is what makes not pygmies but moral giants. And Christ calls us to be giants, not pygmies.

WHY SO MUCH MORAL DECAY?

Troubled by what is happening to our moral standards today, people are asking, "What's happening? Why is there so much crime, immorality, and dishonesty among us?"

There is no one final answer, but one thing that is wrong is that we have forgotten one of the most important words in our vocabulary—that short but powerful word—*no*.

Someone wrote the following testimony to the word *no*:

> *There is something triumphantly final about a positive No! It clicks into place in the mind like a great lock turning, shutting out doubts and hesitancies, barring forever the weaker alternatives. Thunderous negatives have played a dramatic part in our nation's history. "No taxation without representation!" "Millions for defense but not one cent for tribute!" Again and again No! has been the battle cry of free persons: no to compromise, no to injustice, no to tyranny.*

MEN OF THE BIBLE

We live in a permissive society where much that is evil goes unchallenged. It is not easy to stand up and say no when one is convinced that something is contrary to the holy will of God. But exactly that is what is necessary. The Bible offers many examples of people who were able to say no at a crucial time in their lives.

Abraham said no to the natural impulse to spare his son,

Isaac (Hebr. 11:17). Moses said no to the impulse to stay in the affluence and security of Pharoah's household (Hebr. 11:24-26). Joseph said no when tempted by Potiphar's wife (Gen. 39:9). Daniel's companions said no to the temptation to save their lives by bowing before the image Nebuchadnezzar had set up (Dan. 3:16-18). Jesus said no when tempted by Satan. All of us face sin and evil each day of our lives. But God has not left us alone. He has given us the ability to discern evil and the power to resist it by saying no. This grace to say no is one that must be cultivated, not with a hard, unyielding stubbornness, but with the joy of knowing that it is because we have said yes to Jesus that we can and must say no to Satan. "No man can serve two masters," said Jesus.

We need more men like St. Athanasius, the great defender of the Trinitarian faith. When told that the whole world was against him, he replied simply, "Then I shall stand, alone if need be, against the world!" Like the hosts of saints and martyrs before him, Athanasius was able to say no to the world because he had first said yes to Jesus as Lord. From Him—and Him alone—comes the power to say no to evil.

SAYING "NO" IS A BY-PRODUCT

All this talk about saying no to Satan could give us the impression that the main business of Christianity is to say no. But that is not its big concern. That is a by-product. Christianity's big concern is to enable us to say yes to God in Christ. Christianity never says no, except as a reflection of a much higher yes to Jesus. It is Jesus who helps us prioritize, place first things first in life, and gives us the power to say no to that which would betray Him and destroy our self-respect.

The Christian life begins with a renunciation, a rejection, a "breathing and spitting" upon the devil, but it does not end there. The Christian life cannot be built solely on "no's" and "don'ts." You have to say yes to something; you have to be for something; you have to go beyond negative expulsion of evil to positive affirmation of goodness. The Christian no to evil is the by-product of a higher yes to Jesus.

REPENTANCE IS SAYING "NO"

When Jesus calls on us to repent, He is calling on us to say no to sin because we have said yes to God in Christ Jesus. We hear a lot today about the power of positive thinking. Let me tell you one thing: There is just as much power in negative thinking especially when it is directed against sin and evil. Negative thinking is the ability to say no to evil and wrong.

THE EXORCISMS IN BAPTISM: "NO" TO SIN

The Christian life begins in Baptism with the exorcisms where the person who is being received into the faith is called upon, before all else, to renounce the evil one and all his works.

In the early Church the one being baptized was not only required to say no to the devil; he was also required to "breathe and spit" on him three times as a symbol that he had totally repudiated the old, sinful lifestyle so that he might now walk with Jesus "in newness of life" (Rom. 6:4).

The Christian life begins with a firm no to the lifestyle of the devil. We need to remember this. We cannot remain Christians if we do not keep saying no to temptation as we go through life. And—mark you—one cannot say no to the devil unless one has first spoken a big, powerful yes to Jesus. The power to be able to say no to evil comes from that big yes which we spoke to Jesus in Baptism and which we continue to say to Him each day as we "commit ourselves and one another and our whole life to Christ our God."

Keep saying no to the *logismoi* of the evil one. You have to if you have truly said yes to Jesus.

The following prayer summarizes what we have been saying:

Yes, Jesus. Yes to Your love. Yes to the gift of salvation. Yes to Your knock on the door of my heart seeking entrance. Yes to Your forgiveness. Yes to the Holy Spirit within me Who enables me to keep saying no to the temptations of the evil one. Thank you, Jesus, for the great protection I experience when I am enabled by Your grace to speak that tiny but powerful word no. Amen.

THE PRINCE AND THE HARLOT

St. John the Dwarf told the following story to illustrate how we can and must keep saying *no* to Satan:

In one town there lived a beautiful woman, a harlot who had many lovers. A prince suggested to this woman that he would take her to wife if she would promise to live honourably and faithfully in wedlock. She promised, and the prince took her to his court and married her. Discovering this, her former lovers plotted to bring her back to her old ways with them. They did not dare to confront the prince, but gathered behind the palace and began whistling. The woman heard the whistling and recognized it. She quickly blocked her ears and hid herself in an inner room of the palace, locking the door behind her, and was thus preserved from the new temptation. St. John explained this story thus: the harlot is the soul, her lovers are the passions, the prince is Christ, the inner room is the heavenly court, the inner closet of the heart, and the lovers who whistle and entice her are the demons. If the soul is constantly turned from its passions and flees God-ward, the passions and demons will take flight and flee from it.

DON'T LEAVE FOOD AROUND FOR THE FLIES

Eldress Gabriella, who ministered to lepers in India, claimed that *logismoi*, evil thoughts, are like flies that enter an empty room. If there is nothing for them to feed on, nothing to attract them, they will leave.

Can you think of some things in our minds and hearts that attract flies and make them want to stay? If there are, they need to be exorcised.

St. Symeon the New Theologian considered the guarding of the heart against *logismoi* as essential for growing in our relationship to Christ. He wrote:

> *In short, if you do not guard your intellect you cannot attain purity of heart, so as to be counted worthy to see God (cf. Matt 5:18). Without such watchfulness you cannot become poor in spirit, or grieve, or hunger and thirst after righteousness, or be truly merciful, or pure in heart, or a peacemaker, or be persecuted for the sake of justice (cf. Matt 5:3-10). To speak generally, it is impossible to acquire all the other virtues except through watchfulness.*

ALWAYS BE "ON PATROL"

St. Symeon goes on to say, "...the intellect keeps watch over the heart when it prays; it should always be on patrol within the heart...." These words should capture our attention, "The mind should always be *on patrol* within the heart." Because of our Lord's injunction to "cleanse the inside of the cup so that the outside may also be clean" (Matt. 23:26), he goes on to say that the Church Fathers "abandoned all other forms of spiritual labor and concentrated wholly on this one task of guarding the heart, convinced that through this practice they would also possess every other virtue, whereas without watchfulness no virtue could be firmly established." Without watchfulness there can be no purity of heart, without which no one can see God. Writing on the importance of guarding the heart, St. Symeon the New Theologian said, "For someone who desires spiritual rebirth, the first step towards the light is to...guard the heart; for it is impossible otherwise to curtail the passions."

WHY ALL THE EMPHASIS ON WATCHFULNESS?

The Church Fathers emphasized watchfulness greatly because they took seriously what Jesus said:

> *The eye is the lamp of the body, so if your whole eye is sound, your whole body will be full of light. But if your eye is not sound, your whole body will be full of darkness, if then the light in you is darkness, how great is that darkness (Matt. 6:22,23).*

It is safe to say that the whole *Philokalia* is based on the above verse as well as in Proverbs 4:23, "Guard your heart with all vigilance, for from it flow the issues of life."

The eye of the soul is the mind and the heart. These serve as the soul's window through which we can come to see and know God. It is through the eye of the soul that the light of God's presence shines in us and we are able to see spiritually. But Satan is always working through *logismoi* to darken, obscure and even destroy the eye of the soul, this window to God, so as to prevent us from seeing God and to get us to focus on other things which turn out to be false gods or idols. "If your whole eye is sound, your whole body will be full of light" (Matt. 6:2). But "if the light in you is darkness, your whole body will be full of darkness and how great is that darkness."

Through vigilance and prayer the spiritual eye must be kept single and pure; for it is through the eye of the soul that we see God.

CLOSE THE DOOR OF YOUR CELL

St. John of the Ladder offers the following advice on guarding the heart:

> *Close the door of your tongue to speech, and your inner gate to evil spirits. Ascend into a watchtower – if you know how to – and observe how and when and whence, and in what numbers and what form, the robbers try to break in and steal your grapes.... Where thieves see royal weapons at the ready, they do not attack the place lightly. Similarly, spiritual robbers do not lightly try to plunder the person who has enshrined prayer within his heart.*

SCRUTINIZE YOURSELF DAILY

St. Gregory Palamas suggests that if we scrutinize our thoughts daily by guarding the heart, God will not have to scrutinize us when we appear before Him:

> *Do not leave any part of your soul or body unwatched. In this way you will master the evil spirits that assail you and you will boldly present yourself to Him who examines hearts and minds (cf. Ps. 7:9); and He will not scrutinize you, for you will have already scrutinized yourself. As St. Paul says, "If we judged ourselves we would not be judged" (1 Cor. 11:31).*

How can we scrutinize ourselves?

Daily self-examination combined with repentance and confession constitute the best preparation we can make for the Second Coming of Jesus when He will come to judge the world. In the words of St. Gregory, "He will not scrutinize you if you have already scrutinized yourself."

Another way of scrutinizing ourselves is by reading God's

Word each day. God's Word is like a mirror in which we see ourselves as we are and as God wants us to be. Daily scrutinizing through self-examination, the reading of God's Word and repentance is how the Christian practices "quality control" in life.

CLING TO THE LORD IN PRAYER

Another father, St. Theodoros the Great Ascetic, emphasizes the importance of clinging to the Lord in prayer as we guard the heart:

> *It is impossible to speak of all the various snares they set on the spiritual path, making use of the senses, the reason, the intellect – in fact, of everything that exists. If He who carries the lost sheep on His shoulders (cf. Luke 15:5) did not in His infinite care protect those who turn to Him, not a single soul would escape.*
>
> *Three things are needed in order to overcome these obstacles. The first and most important thing is to look to God with our whole soul, to ask for help from His hand, and to put all our trust in Him, knowing full well that without His assistance we shall inevitably be dragged away from Him....*

We call Him to our side and ask for help from His hand through the Jesus Prayer.

FOUR STEPS TO LIFT THE MIND TO HEAVEN

St. Thalassios describes the four steps that will lift the intellect to heaven. He writes, "Stillness, prayer, love and self-control are a four-horsed chariot bearing the intellect to heaven."

St. Maximus the Confessor reflects on how thoughts that are allowed to enter the mind, inevitably lead the body to fall into sin:

But when you see that your intellect is occupied with thoughts of sin, and you do not check it, you may be sure that before very long your body, too, will fall into those sins.

He brings us back to the words of Proverbs 4:23, "Guard your heart with all vigilance, for from it flow the issues of life."

WATCH AND PRAY

Another father of the *Philokalia,* St. Peter of Damaskos, says that without attentiveness and watchfulness of the intellect (mind), we cannot be saved and rescued from the devil, who walks around "like a roaring lion, seeking whom he may devour" (1 Peter 5:8). For this reason the Lord often said to His disciples, "Watch and pray lest you enter into temptation. The spirit indeed is willing, but the flesh is weak" (Matt. 26:41).

DESTROY *LOGISMOI* AT THEIR FIRST APPEARANCE

Also from the *Philokalia,* St. Philotheos of Sinai, calls on us to destroy hostile thoughts *at their first appearance.* "It is by means of thoughts (*logismoi*) that the spirits of evil wage a secret war against the soul," he wrote. He also counsels us against pride which comes to us if we manage to succeed once in a while in resisting evil thoughts, for pride always "goeth before a fall." He writes:

If with the Lord's help you cleanse your heart and uproot sin – struggling for the knowledge that is more divine and seeing in your intellect things invisible to most people – you must not on this account be arrogant towards anyone. For an angel, being incorporeal, is more pure and full of spiritual knowledge than any other created thing; yet it was an angel who, in exalting himself, fell like lightning from heaven. Thus his pride was reckoned by God as impurity.

CONCENTRATE THE SCATTERED INTELLECT THROUGH THE THOUGHT OF DEATH AND THE REMEMBRANCE OF JESUS

St. Philotheos urges us to concentrate our scattered intellect through the thought of death and the remembrance of Jesus.

> *Chastise your soul with the thought of death, and through the remembrance of Jesus Christ concentrate your scattered intellect.*

The thought of death combined with the remembrance of Jesus concentrates the scattered mind, says Philotheos. One person does this by practicing what he calls the "death pose." He explains that this is a Yoga pose that simulates death. One lies on one's back on the floor or on one's bed with legs slightly apart and toes relaxed with the arms crossed over the chest. In this pose, one can meditate on one's own death. As one does this, I can assure you that the wandering intellect will be greatly concentrated and focused. Monks practice this by constructing their own coffin and sleeping in it periodically.

"Concentrate your *wandering* intellect," says Philotheos.

The word for wandering in Greek is *plane*. The English word "planet" comes from the Greek word *plane*. According to the ancients, a planet was always wandering in the night sky. This is because planets were never in the same place two nights in a row. They appeared to be wanderers in the night sky. The *Philokalia* Fathers were very concerned about the inability of the mind to stay focused; they were greatly concerned about the ease with which Satan was able to distract the mind and lead it into illusion and delusion. It is something to which Jesus spoke in Luke 21:34-35:

> *But take heed to yourselves lest your hearts be weighed down with dissipation and drunkenness and the cares of this life, and that day come upon you sud-*

denly like a snare; for it will come upon all who dwell upon the face of the whole earth.

In Matthew 6:25 and 6:27 Jesus uses the Greek word *merimnao* for the cares and anxieties of the world (*logismoi*). This word means literally "to run around in circles with the mind." We spend an enormous amount of time running around in mental circles with anxieties and cares that never come to pass or are unreal. And this prevents us from focusing on the real and important. The extreme of this wandering state of mind is mental illness, where the person is unable to focus on anything but is completely anxious and fearful. That is why the *Philokalia* calls on us to combine *hysychia*, stillness, with the Jesus Prayer through which we become more internally quiet, less anxious, less fragmented and more focused.

St. Philotheos directs us also to use violence against such fragmented thoughts (*logismoi*):

> *You must direct your wrath only against the demons for they wage war upon us through our thoughts and are full of anger against us. As regards the manner of the hourly warfare within us, listen and act accordingly. Combine prayer with inner watchfulness, for watchfulness purifies prayer, while prayer purifies watchfulness. It is through unceasing watchfulness that we can perceive what is entering into us and can to some extent close the door against it, calling upon our Lord Jesus Christ to repel our malevolent adversaries. Attentiveness obstructs the demons by rebutting them; and Jesus, when invoked, disperses them together with all their fantasies.*

ADDITIONAL COUNSELS ON COPING WITH *LOGISMOI*

St. Philotheos goes on to describe the prize that the prayerfully watchful heart gains:

> *Let us go forward with the heart completely attentive and the soul fully conscious. For if attentiveness and prayer are daily joined together, they become like Elijah's fire-bearing chariot (cf. 2 Kgs 2:11), raising us to heaven. What do I mean? A spiritual heaven, with sun, moon and stars, is formed in the blessed heart of one who has reached a state of watchfulness, or who strives to attain it; for such a heart, as a result of mystical contemplation and ascent, is enabled to contain within itself the uncontainable God.*

St. Hesychios adds that prayerful watchfulness reduces the evil in us but requires certain forcefulness. He writes that it should be a *forceful* watchfulness:

> *Let us pass all the hours of the day in the guarding of the intellect, for by doing this we shall with God's help and with a certain forcefulness be able to quell and reduce the evil in us. For the spiritual life, through which the kingdom of heaven is given, does indeed require a certain forcefulness (cf. Matt. 11:12).*

Such a forceful watchfulness combined with prayer serves to "reduce the evil in us," says St. Hesychios.

People today are so eager to reduce their fat intake that they will even join health clubs and work strenuously on treadmills to do so. The Church Fathers did not have to be concerned with obesity since fasting was so much a part of their lifestyle. The thing that concerned them most was "to reduce the evil" in them through forceful, prayerful watchfulness. "Watch and pray that you enter not into temptation. For the spirit is willing, but the body is weak," said Jesus.

St. Evagrios points out the blessed result of guarding the mind and heart in inner tranquility:

> *Stand on guard and protect your intellect from thoughts while you pray. Then your intellect will complete its prayer and continue in the tranquility that is natural to it.*

Watchfuless and prayer return the soul to its natural inner tranquility, says St. Evagrios.

"PUT ON THE WHOLE ARMOR OF GOD"

St. Paul described the inner battle every Christian is called to wage against *logismoi*, evil thoughts, when he wrote in Ephesians 6:10-12:

> *Finally, be strong in the Lord and in the strength of his might. Put on the whole armor of God, that you may be able to stand against the wiles of the devil. For we are not contending against flesh and blood, but against the principalities, against the powers, against the world rulers of this present darkness, against the spiritual hosts of wickedness in the heavenly places.*

In other words, St. Paul, like Jesus Himself, believed in a spiritual world inhabited by principalities, powers and spiritual hosts (demons), headed by Satan himself.

INNER POLLUTION

It is for this reason that the ancient writers of the *Philokalia* emphasize the importance of guarding the mind and the heart. We talk much about how the world is being damaged today by pollution, but little is said of the fact that the outer pollution of man and earth originates from the inner pollution of the mind and heart. It is here that we need to eliminate the spiritual pollution by practicing inner quality control, screening carefully the thoughts that we allow to enter our minds, discriminating between good and evil thoughts, encouraging and strengthening the good as we discourage and expel the bad thoughts.

KNOW THYSELF THROUGH PRAYERFUL INTROSPECTION

This is where the Jesus Prayer comes to our assistance. It enables us to observe and control what goes on inside us. Through prayer and stillness we observe carefully what is happening within us. We get to know our fears, our anxieties, as well as our hopes and aspirations. We come to know ourselves in a deep and profound way. We discover the image of God in us, but we discover also what the *Philokalia* calls the "passions" in us. Once we realize how serious our inner condition is, we call on God to take charge of our lives. We beseech Him to empower us to resist the evil one. We call Him to our side through the Jesus Prayer, "Lord Jesus, Son of God, have mercy on me."

CONSTANT WEEDING OF HARMFUL *LOGISMOI*

It is much like tending a garden. Flowers are beautiful but they require constant care. Once the weeds take over, there is no more garden. It becomes an untamed wilderness. Hence the need daily to pull the weeds and tend the soil. By discouraging and renouncing the evil, we are encouraging the good. It doesn't take much neglect for evil to take over. Just sit back and do nothing and evil will triumph.

As G. K. Chesterton said, "If you leave a thing alone, you leave it to a torrent of change. If you leave a white post alone, it will soon be a black post. If you particularly want it to be white, you must be always painting it again."

CHANGING CHANNELS

It is much the same as watching television. We have to constantly "change channels," screening out the bad and being very selective about what we allow in through the senses. This is why the *Philokalia* urges us to "cut off" the incipient evil thought (*logismoi*) immediately with the Jesus Prayer. This is how it works. By diverting our thought to God, the Jesus Prayer defuses the power of the bad thought and expels it from the mind. This should be done immediately because once the bad thought had proceeded to the stage of assent and consent, it is very difficult to stop it. Hence the importance of continually "changing channels," selecting another channel when we are presented with thoughts that are not edifying. "Put on the armor of God," says St. Paul. The "armor of God" that enables us to do this is the power that resides in the name of Jesus: "Lord Jesus, Son of God, have mercy on me, help me."

If we do not control our thoughts, then they will control us. They will victimize us. We will be at their mercy. Self-mastery requires constant vigilance and prayer, *proseuche* and *prosoche*. That is why the *Philokalia* calls those who seek union with God "spiritual wrestlers." They call on us to exert ourselves 100% and yet, at the same time, to relax totally and rely on the grace of God to open the door of salvation for us. And since Jesus Himself is the door, He will open it.

COUNTER-SPEAKING

The Church Fathers encourage us to talk back to evil thoughts when they attack. They call this method *antirrhesis* (counter-speaking). When Jesus was tempted by the devil, He talked back to the devil with quotations from Scripture (Luke 4:1-13). Through counter-speaking we close the door on the voice of Satan and open the door to the voice of God. The Desert Fathers practiced the method of counter-speaking (*antirrhesis*) as the following story illustrates.

> *They used to say concerning an elder, "While he was living in his cell a brother came by night to visit him. He heard him inside disputing and saying, 'Oh, that's enough, get out,' and then, 'Come to me, friend.' The brother entered and said to him, 'Abba, to whom were you speaking?' And he said, 'I was driving away my wicked thoughts and calling on the good ones.'"*

He was counter-speaking, speaking harshly to the *logismoi* that were assaulting him *(antirrhesis)*.

AMMA SYNCLETICA

Amma Syncletica of Egypt (390-470) offers another example of *antirrhesis*. She writes:

> *When the devil tempts us to be proud, he hides our sins from us, but when he tempts us to lose hope he places our sins before us and suggests: "Since you have committed all these sins, what forgiveness will there be?" (None!) To another he says, "Since you have been so greedy, how can you obtain salvation?" (Impossible!)*

How do we respond to such dismal demonic hopelessness? This is the counsel Amma Syncletica offers:

> *Souls...that have been thus shaken should be comforted in the following way – in fact, it is essential to speak to them in this way – "Rehab was a prostitute, but she was saved through faith; Paul was a persecutor, but he became a chosen instrument; Matthew was a tax collector, but no one is ignorant of the grace granted him; and the thief stole and murdered, but he was the first to open the door of Paradise. Keeping these people in mind, therefore, do not give up hope for your own soul."*

ST. MAKARIOS ON COUNTER-SPEAKING

St. Makarios of Egypt also offers counsel on how to counter-speak to Satan when he comes to tempt us:

> *It often happens that Satan will insidiously commune with you in your heart and say: "Think of the evil you have done; your soul is full of lawlessness, you are weighed down by many grievous sins." Do not let him deceive you when he does this and do not be led to despair.... After gaining admission through the fall, evil has the power to commune at all times with the soul..., and so to suggest sinful actions to it. You should answer it: "I have God's written assurance, for He says: 'I desire, not the sinner's death, but that he should return through repentance and live'" (cf. Ezek. 33:11). What was the purpose of His descent to earth except to save sinners, to bring light to those in darkness and life to the dead?*

AN EXAMPLE OF COUNTER-SPEAKING TO SATAN

An example of counter-speaking is the following conversation that portrays Satan speaking to us and God counter-speaking to Satan in our behalf. For all the negative suggestions Satan directs to us, God has a positive answer:

Satan says: "It's impossible."
God says: "All things are possible" (Luke 18:27).

Satan says: "You're too tired."
God says: "I will give you rest" (Matt. 11:28-30).

Satan says: "Nobody really loves you."
God says: "I love you" (John 3:16 – John 13:34).

Satan says:	"You can't go on. You're at the end of your rope."
God says:	"My grace is sufficient" (2 Cor. 12:9 - Psalm 91:15).
Satan says:	"It doesn't make sense. There's nothing but darkness ahead."
God says:	"I will direct your steps" (Proverbs 3:5-6).
Satan says:	"You can't do it."
God says:	"You can do all things in Me" (Phil. 4:13).
Satan says:	"It's not worth it."
God says:	"It will be worth it" (Romans 8:28).
Satan says:	"There is no hope for you. Your sins are too many."
God says:	"I forgive you" (1 John 1:9 - Romans 8:1).
Satan says:	"You can't manage."
God says:	"I will supply all your needs" (Phil. 4:19).
Satan says:	"You should be afraid."
God says:	"I have not given you a spirit of fear" (2 Tim 1:7).
Satan says:	"You are too worried and frustrated. You will fail."
God says:	"Cast all your cares on ME (1 Peter 5:7).
Satan says:	"You don't have enough faith."
God says:	"I've given everyone a measure of faith" (Romans 12:3).
Satan says:	"You're not smart enough."
God says:	"I give you wisdom" (1 Cor. 1:30).

Satan says: "You are all alone. Everyone has forsaken you."
God says: "I will never leave you or forsake you" (Heb. 13:5).

THE JESUS PRAYER GATHERS THE SCATTERED MIND

The most effective way of counter-speaking to evil thoughts is by invoking the all-powerful name of Jesus through the Jesus Prayer. The name of Jesus, prayed with the mind in the heart, has been called a "quasi-sacrament of the presence (of Jesus)" by Olivier Clement. The Jesus Prayer brings the fullness of the presence of Christ with it. As we know, the Jesus Prayer may be shortened from "Lord Jesus, Son of God, have mercy on me" to "Lord Jesus" or to simply the name that is above every name, "Jesus! Jesus! Jesus!" The all-powerful name is a great weapon; it is part of the "armor of God" against evil thoughts. It is called "a weapon stronger than any other in heaven or on earth, a gift of God" (Bishop Ignatii). It eliminates the deafening static of the *logismoi*, enabling us to hear the voice of God speaking to us. It restores calm and causes joy to rise in us. It keeps the mind focused on Jesus and disperses all irrelevant thoughts. The name of Jesus, invoked prayerfully, writes St. Philotheos of Sinai, "gathers together your scattered intellect."

A TRAFFIC POLICEMAN ON DUTY

Through the Jesus Prayer, Christ controls our minds and hearts. He becomes like the traffic policeman who stands on duty at the intersection of busy streets and directs the flowing tide of autos and pedestrians (*logismoi*). When there is no traffic policeman at the post, we have chaos and collisions. Pandemonium reigns. Not so when we call upon the Savior to direct the traffic of thoughts in our minds and hearts. Then there is coordination, harmony, balance, peace and joy in our lives.

FASTEN THE MIND ON JESUS

To silence the mind is an extremely difficult task. It is hard to keep the mind from thinking, thinking, thinking, fantasizing, fantasizing, fantasizing, forever producing thoughts (*logismoi*) in a never-ending stream. The Fathers of the *Philokalia* have taught us the way to control the mind. It is by using one thought to rid ourselves of all other thoughts that seek to crowd the mind. That one thought is the Jesus Prayer or just the name "Jesus" prayerfully invoked. By fastening the mind on the powerful name of Jesus, we are enabled to close the mind to the voice of Satan and open it to the voice of God, keeping at bay all the demonic voices that seek to intrude. "He who has achieved (inner) stillness has arrived at the essence of the Christian faith," wrote St. John Climacus. The goal of the Jesus Prayer is to achieve such stillness by "standing in the presence of God with the mind in the heart."

BIND THE MIND WITH ONE THOUGHT

"To stop the continual jostling of your thoughts," writes St. Theophan, "you must bind the mind with one thought, or the thought of One only"—the thought of the Lord Jesus. "The mind is a dangerous place," someone said. "You should not go into it alone. Take God with you." Take the Jesus Prayer with you.

HOW THE JESUS PRAYER HELPS US RESIST *LOGISMOI* (EVIL THOUGHTS)

The Fathers of the *Philokalia* have much to say about how the Jesus Prayer can help us resist evil thoughts. Following are a few of their thoughts:

> *When combined with watchfulness and deep understanding, the Jesus Prayer will erase from our*

heart even those thoughts rooted there against our will.

—St. Hesychios

Just as it is impossible to cross the sea without a boat, so it is impossible to repulse the provocation of an evil thought without invoking Jesus Christ. Rebuttal bridles evil thoughts, but the invocation of Jesus Christ drives them from the heart.

—St. Hesychios

Those who lack experience should know that it is only through the unceasing watchfulness of our intellect and the constant invocation of Jesus Christ, our Creator and God, that we, coarse and cloddish in mind and body as we are, can overcome our bodiless and invisible enemies; for not only are they subtle, swift, malevolent and skilled in malice, but they have an experience in warfare gained over all the years since Adam.

—St. Hesychios

Watchfulness and the Jesus Prayer, as I have said, mutually reinforce one another; for close attentiveness goes with constant prayer, while prayer goes with close watchfulness and attentiveness of intellect.

—St. Hesychios

The name of Jesus should be repeated over and over in the heart as flashes of lightning are repeated over and over in the sky before rain. Those who have experience of the intellect and of inner warfare know this very well. We should wage this spiritual warfare with a precise sequence: first, with attentiveness; then,

> *when we perceive the hostile thought attacking, we should strike at it angrily in the heart, cursing it as we do so; thirdly, we should direct our prayer against it, concentrating the heart through the invocation of Jesus Christ, so that the demonic fantasy may be dispersed at once....*
>
> —St. Hesychios

> *The single-phrased Jesus Prayer destroys and consumes the deceits of the demons. For when we invoke Jesus, the Son of God, constantly and tirelessly, He does not allow them to project in the mind's mirror even the first hint of their infiltration....*
>
> *It is through unceasing prayer that the mind is cleansed of the dark clouds, the tempests of the demons. And when it is cleansed, the divine light of Jesus cannot but shine in it....*
>
> —St. Hesychios

St. Philotheos of Sinai commends the invocation of the Holy Name (the Jesus Prayer) because it not only has the power to concentrate the scattered mind but also enables it to maintain continued mindfulness of God in stillness at heart.

St. Thalassios writes:

> *Impell your intellect continually to prayer and you will destroy the evil thoughts that beset your heart.*

St. Hesychios reminds us that with the Jesus Prayer we are never alone when we battle the *logismoi*:

> *The devil, with all his powers, "walks about like a roaring lion, seeking whom he may devour" (1 Pet. 5:8). So you must never relax your attentiveness of*

> *heart, your watchfulness, your power of rebuttal or your prayer to Jesus Christ our God. You will not find a greater help than Jesus in all your life, for He alone, as God, knows the deceitful ways of the demons, their subtlety and their guile.*
>
> *Let your soul, then, trust in Christ, let it call on Him and never fear; for it fights, not alone, but with the aid of a mighty King, Jesus Christ, Creator of all that is, both bodiless and embodied, visible and invisible.*
>
> —St. Hesychios

Abba Philemon tells the following instructive story about resisting *logismoi*. It is a story that highlights the importance of the Jesus Prayer.

> *A brother named John came from the coast to Father Philemon and, clasping his feet, said to him: "What shall I do to be saved? For my intellect vacillates to and fro and strays after all the wrong things." After a pause, the father replied: "This is one of the outer passions and it stays with you because you still have not acquired a perfect longing for God. The warmth of this longing and of the knowledge of God has not yet come to you." The brother said to him: "What shall I do, father?" Abba Philemon replied: "Meditate inwardly for a while, deep in your heart; for this can cleanse your intellect of these things." The brother, not understanding what was said, asked the Elder: "What is inward meditation, father?" The Elder replied: "Keep watch in your heart; and with watchfulness say in your mind with awe and trembling: ' Lord Jesus Christ, have mercy upon me.' For this is the advice which the blessed Diadochos gave to beginners."*

Archimandrite Sophrony advises us not to become discouraged when, despite the Jesus Prayer, the mind continues to be besieged by evil thoughts. He sees meaning in this as he writes in his book, *His Life is Mine*:

> *Often when we would pray the Jesus Prayer the mind is besieged by inopportune thoughts of every kind which distract the attention from the heart. Our prayer seems fruitless because the mind is not participating in the invocation of the Lord's Name and only our lips continue mechanically to repeat the words. But there is meaning in this influx of untimely thoughts: our prayer becomes as it were a shaft of light focused on the dark places of our inner life, revealing to us the passions or attachments occupying the soul. We learn what we have to fight against; we see the iniquities that sway us. And then we call all the more urgently on the Name of God, and our repentance is intensified, Lord Jesus Christ, Son of God, have mercy upon me.**

In summary, the Fathers of the *Philokalia* tell us that there is no more powerful weapon on earth or in heaven than the Jesus Prayer when it comes to resisting evil thoughts. In fact, the Jesus Prayer has been described as "the spiritual heart of the *Philokalia*" (Dr. Andrew Louth).

Thus, the tried and tested method for resisting evil thoughts in the *Philokalia* is *prosoche* (vigilance) and *proseuche* (prayer). "Watch and pray," said Jesus, "that you enter not into temptation. For the spirit is willing but the flesh is weak."

IT IS NOT IN OUR POWER TO UPROOT *LOGISMOI*

While it is incumbent upon us to resist evil thoughts, to struggle against them, to strike back, to counter-speak and to continue to resist them, it is not within our power to uproot

*SVS Press. Crestwood, N.Y., 1977.

them. This can only be done only by the power of the Triune God. And He grants the victory to those who demonstrate their good intention by vigilant, forceful resisting, counter-speaking and prayer. St. Anthony complained to God one day because He felt that God was not helping him when he was being assailed by *logismoi*. "Where were You, Lord? Why didn't You help me?" asked Anthony. And the Lord said, "I was waiting to see what you would do. Once I saw that you were resisting, I stepped in to help you."

PRAYER AND VIGILANCE

To be an effective gatekeeper at the door of the mind, the Church Fathers emphasize the importance of prayer and vigilance. No one can be truly vigilant as a gatekeeper of the mind without the power that comes from prayer. One of the elders said, "Pray attentively (with vigilance) and you will soon straighten out your thoughts." St. Philotheos of Sinai defined the relationship between prayer and watchfulness as follows:

> *You must direct your wrath only against the demons, for they wage war upon us through our thoughts and are full of anger against us. As regards the manner of the hourly warfare within us, listen and act accordingly. Combine prayer with inner watchfulness, for watchfulness purifies prayer, while prayer purifies watchfulness. It is through unceasing watchfulness that we can perceive what is entering into us and can to some extent close the door against it, calling upon our Lord Jesus Christ to repel our malevolent adversaries. Attentiveness obstructs the demons by rebutting them; and Jesus, when invoked, disperses them together with all their fantasies.*

St. Syncletike recommends the following:

> *It is necessary constantly to clean out the house and to see that nothing harmful to the soul penetrates into the chambers of the soul. (How?) By censing these places with the divine incense of prayer. For as poisonous creatures are sent away by certain other strong poisons, so also are evil thoughts banished by prayer and fasting.*

A MENTAL SHAMPOO

Another way to resist evil thoughts is by taking a mental shampoo each day. Bad thoughts soil the mind. No matter how hard we try to keep our thoughts pure and good, our minds become sullied by the things we see and hear, just as our hands get soiled from the things we touch and handle. Fortunately, it isn't fatal. In fact, as every mother knows, the cure is very simple. In the evening when the children come in grimy from play, she simply plops them into the bathtub and scrubs them clean.

Having a bad thought occur to someone isn't fatal spiritually. It simply means one needs a mental or spiritual bath, what the Bible calls "the renewing of your mind"(Eph. 4:23). It is not something we are to do just once. It is something that needs to be done each day. We can take a mental or spiritual bath each day by spending time with God in self-examination and asking Him to cleanse our mind by seeking His forgiveness and saturating our mind with His Word.

Dr. Sara Jordan of the Lahey Clinic, an outstanding medical doctor, expressed this same truth when she said, "Every day give your mind a good shampoo." Part of this daily "shampoo" according to the monastic discipline of the Church is for the spiritual child to reveal to his *geronta* (spiritual father) not only his sins but also the thoughts (*logismoi*) that enter his mind long before they become outward acts. This is considered to be a prophylactic inner cleansing. It is a saying of the Church Fathers that, "A monk stands or falls by his thoughts. If he discloses his thoughts, the angels rejoice. If he conceals them, God's grace will be hidden from him."

As long as we keep our thoughts concealed, they exert power over us; they control us. But when we disclose our thoughts to God and to a spiritual father or friend, they lose their hold on us. We control them. This is also what psychotherapy is all about.

WHEN THOUGHTS ARE CONCEALED THEY EXERT POWER OVER US

Confessing *logismoi* to a spiritual elder makes us better able to resist them. We read about this in the *Gerontikon*, a collection of sayings of the Desert Fathers:

> *If impure thoughts trouble you, do not hide them, but tell them at once to your spiritual father and condemn them. The more a person conceals his thoughts, the more they multiply and gain strength. But an evil thought, when revealed, is immediately destroyed. If you hide things, they have great power over you, but if you could only speak of them before God, in the presence of another, then they will often wither away, and lose their power.*

This is profound spiritual psychotherapy.

John Cassian adds:

> *An evil thought sheds its danger when it is brought into the open…like the most foul serpent which has been dragged out of its dark subterranean lair into the light… (it) retreats, disgraced and denounced. Its dangerous promptings hold sway in us (only) as long as they are concealed in the heart.*

Thus, through the disclosure to an elder not just of sins but also of thoughts before they become sins, the *logismoi* lose the appalling power they have when concealed.

When the young monk appears before his spiritual father each evening to manifest his thoughts, this daily regimen of accountability—greatly demanding as it is—helps him make rapid progress toward purity of heart.

Bishop Ware said once that "nothing gives…evil thoughts such power over us as to nourish them and hide them in our hearts unconfessed. But, once brought into the open, they become powerless over us." Sigmund Freud discovered this truth as he listened patiently to persons who were mentally troubled. The disclosure of thoughts, formerly concealed, brings healing.

"WHY ARE YOU STILL CARRYING HER?"

The Desert Fathers tell the following story:

Two monks on a pilgrimage came to the ford of a river. There they saw a girl dressed in all her finery, obviously not knowing what to do since the river was high and she did not want to spoil her clothes. Without more ado, one of the monks took her on his back, carried her across and put her down on dry ground on the other side. Then the monks continued on their way. But the other monk after an hour started complaining, "Surely it is not right to touch a woman; it is against the commandments to have close contact with women. How could you go against the rules of monks?" The monk who had carried the girl walked along silently, but finally he remarked, "I set her down by the river an hour ago, why are you still carrying her?" One way of not allowing evil thoughts to control us is by not continuing to carry them in our mind, by disclosing them to a spiritual father or friend.

EMPTY YOUR MIND OF SINFUL THOUGHTS

It is important that we empty our mind regularly, discarding unwholesome thoughts. As many of us accumulate junk in the attic, intending to clean it out some day, but never getting around to it, so we allow our minds to accumulate vast impedimenta of resentments, fears, inferiority feelings, gripes, grudges, etc.

When I come home at night, one of the first things I do is wash my hands, sending down the drain the dirt that has accumulated during the day. In exactly the same manner, we need to clean out our minds.

A noted psychologist said, "I am appalled at the multitude of people who have never learned to empty their minds."

One person has what he calls a "vacuum cleaner" prayer: "Dear Lord, by the power of Thy Holy Spirit, draw now from the unseen crannies and crevices of my soul the dust of the world that has settled there."

One Church Father said, "The mind is filled with thoughts that create a gulf between man and God. Empty the mind; in the stillness you will find union with God." "Be still and know that I am God," says the Lord.

Another one of the Fathers said, "Just as it is impossible for a man to see his face in troubled water, so too the soul, unless it be cleansed of alien thoughts, cannot pray to God in contemplation."

Hence the importance of "shampooing" the mind. We shampoo the mind by emptying it of *logismoi* through sharing them with a spiritual elder or mentor. We "shampoo" the mind also by filling it with the Word of God. By studying God's Word and listening to the preaching of the Word in church, the mind is purified and cleansed.

As Jesus told His disciples, "You are already clean because of the Word I have spoken to you" (John 15:3). Studying and listening to the Word of God cleanses and purifies the mind, says Jesus. "Blessed are the pure in heart for they shall see God"

(Matt. 5:8). The greater the inner purity of the mind, the more shall we be able to see God.

St. Maximus the Confessor wrote:

> *If, as St. Paul says, Christ dwells in our hearts through faith (cf. Eph. 3:17), and all the treasures of wisdom and spiritual knowledge are hidden in Him (cf. Col. 2:3), then all the treasures of wisdom and spiritual knowledge are hidden in our hearts. They are revealed to the heart in proportion to our purification....*

Elsewhere, St. Maximus says:

> *Cleanse your intellect from anger, rancor and shameful thoughts, and you will be able to perceive the indwelling of Christ.*

"Blessed are the pure in heart, for they shall see God."

FILL YOUR MIND WITH GOD

As it is important to *empty* our minds of *logismoi,* so it is important to *fill* our minds with holy thoughts, noble *logismoi.* As we empty a glass of air by filling it with water, so we empty the mind of evil thoughts by filling it with God's Word. This is what St. Paul is urging us to do when he writes:

> *Finally, brethren, whatever is true, whatever is honorable, whatever is just, whatever is pure, whatever is lovely, whatever is gracious, if there is any excellence, if there is anything worthy of praise, think about these things (Philippians 4:8).*

A woman went to her doctor one day with a catalog of complaints about her health. After a thorough examination the doctor came to the conclusion that there was nothing physically wrong. He was convinced that the woman's negative outlook was responsible for the way she felt. Bitterness and resentment raged within her mind. The wise doctor took her to his office where there was a shelf of empty bottles. They were all shaped differently. Then he said to her, "I can take any one of these bottles and fill it with enough poison to kill a person, or I can fill a bottle with a medicine that will ease a throbbing headache or fight bacteria. The choice is mine." Then he told her that each day was like an empty bottle. We can choose to fill it with love and life-affirming thoughts, or we can fill it with poisonous thoughts. The choice is ours.

And I do not have to do it all at once. I do not have to change all my thoughts immediately. I can only think one thought at a time anyway. But each day as I study God's Word, I can start filling my mind with God, one thought at a time, one divine promise at a time.

A JAPANESE CUSTOM

An American who visited Japan was a houseguest of a Japanese friend. He learned that the Japanese first take a shower to remove germs from their body. Then, right after the shower, they sit in a hot tub. When asked for the reason for this, the American was told that this is done for the renewing of the mind. So it is that the *Philokalia* Fathers emphasize not just the emptying of the mind of *logismoi*, but also the renewing of the mind by filling it with the Jesus Prayer and God's Word.

HOLY LOGISMOI

St. John of Sinai enumerates some of the holy *logismoi* that can help us crowd out the demonic *logismoi*:

> *There are many activities for an active mind. I mean, meditation on the love of God, on the remembrance of God, on the remembrance of the Kingdom, on the remembrance of the zeal of the holy martyrs, on the*

remembrance of God Himself present, according to the Psalmist who said: "I beheld the Lord ever before me" (Psalm 15:8), on the remembrance of the holy angels, on remembrance of the soul's departure from the body, judgment, sentence and punishment....

When the mind is filled with godly thoughts, there will be no room for evil thoughts. In fact, St. Thalassios writes, "The proper activity of the mind is to be attentive at every moment to the Words of God." Abba Philemon adds that a mind so filled with the Word of God will have no difficulty repelling evil thoughts. He writes:

Pay strict attention to your heart and watch over it, so that it does not give admittance to thoughts that are evil or in any way vain and useless. Without interruption, whether asleep or awake, eating, drinking, or in company, let your heart inwardly and mentally at all times be meditating on the psalms.

Nikitas Stithatos explains that a mind filled with Holy Scripture will harvest ever more exalted divine thoughts:

We pray with the intellect when, as we say prayers and recite psalms, we perceive the meaning hidden in the Holy Scriptures and thence garner in the heart a harvest of ever more exalted divine thoughts. Rapt spiritually by these thoughts into the regions of light, the soul shines with a clear radiance, is further purified, rises wholly to the heavens, and beholds the beauty of the blessings held in store for the saints.

TOLSTOY

An example of this is Leo Tolstoy who was able to expel the demon of deep despondency by filling his mind with the

Word of God. Tolstoy went through a period of deep anxiety. Nothing made sense to him, nothing seemed worthwhile. He even hid rope lest in an unguarded moment he might take his life. And he came out of it, he says, by focusing his thoughts on God. He kept saying over and over to himself, "The eternal God is my refuge," until bit by bit, there was an uprush of hope in him and his heart grew quiet and composed.

That is why one of the Syriac Fathers, Babai, said, "Let the thought of God revolve in your heart more than breath in your nostrils." If a thought of dejection or defeat comes to you, replace it with a thought of confidence from God's Word, as for example: "The Lord is my strength and my salvation. Whom shall I fear?" If a thought of fear and hopelessness comes, replace it with a thought of courage and strength from God's Word: "Why are you cast down, O my soul? Hope thou in God."

When Albert Einstein was asked to give his phone number one day, he looked puzzled for a moment, but then he went over to the nearest phone book and looked it up. Was he forgetful? No! He refused to clutter his mind with inconsequential information. He wished to keep his mind open to receive information that was important to him. And this is exactly what St. John Chrysostom advises when he writes:

> *What is it then to be a fool for Christ? It is to control one's thoughts when they stray out of line. It is to make the mind empty and free so as to be able to offer it in a state of readiness when Christ's teachings are to be assimilated, swept clean for the words of God that it needs to welcome.*

Unclutter your mind and keep it open and ready to welcome God's Word, says Chrysostom. Only then can it bless you and bear fruit.

FINAL THOUGHTS FROM THE CHURCH FATHERS ON *LOGISMOI*

Do not corrupt your flesh with shameful deeds; do not pollute your soul with evil thoughts and the peace of God will descend on you, bringing with it love.

—St. Maximos the Confessor

The heart supplies blood to all the members of the body, down to the smallest capillary. The same thing occurs in the spiritual life. When the heart is free from sin, clean of every passion and of every passionate thought, then all our sensory members will be clean, since they will be supplied by a pure heart.

– *Philokalia*

In storms and squalls we need a pilot, and in this present life we need prayer; for we are susceptible to the provocations of our thoughts, both good and bad. If our thought is full of devotion and love of God, it rules over the passions.

—St. Isaiah the Solitary

Reveal yourself to the Lord in your mind, "For man looks at the outward appearance, but the Lord looks at the heart" (1 Sam. 16:7).

—St. Mark the Ascetic

The Theotokos was a virgin not only in body but also in mind.

—St. Ambrose

Never belittle the significance of your thoughts, for not one escapes God's notice.

—St. Mark the Ascetic

Some brothers once asked Abba Silouan, "What kind of life did you lead, what struggles have you pursued so as to receive this wisdom?" He replied, "Never did I leave a thought in my heart that would offend God."

—Desert Fathers

THE MOST IMPORTANT PART OF THE HOUSE

When building a house, the most important parts are those that one cannot see. Things like paint, wallpaper, and siding are easy to see, but the things one cannot see are the most important: the foundation and the hidden framework of girders, beams, studs and other supports. These are all invisible to the eye, yet they hold the building together.

So it is with us. The most important part of us is that which cannot be seen: the mind, the heart and what we allow to enter them. "Guard your heart with all vigilance, for from it flow the springs of life" (Prov. 4:23).

This requires daily prayer, prayerful vigilance and regular self-examination. In the words of St. Hesychios of the *Philokalia*:

St. Basil the Great, mouthpiece of Christ and pillar of the Church, says that a great help towards not sinning and not committing daily the same faults is for us to review in our conscience at the end of each day what we have done wrong and what we have done right. Job did this with regard both to himself and to his children (cf. Job 1:5). These daily reckonings illumine a man's hour by hour behaviour.

About the Author
Anthony M. Coniaris

Father Anthony M. Coniaris has served at St. Mary's Greek Orthodox Church in Minneapolis, Minnesota, since 1948. Ordained a Deacon in 1950 and a Priest in 1953, he is a native of Boston, Massachusetts, where he attended the Boston Latin School. He is a graduate of the Holy Cross Greek Orthodox Theological Seminary in Brookline, Massachusetts, as well as the Northwestern Theological Seminary in Minneapolis. He has attended postgraduate studies in the fields of religion and psychiatry at the University of Minnesota and at St. John's University in Collegeville, Minnesota.

Father Coniaris has been in charge of Eastern Orthodox student work at the University of Minnesota, where he served on the Council of Religious Advisors. He has served on the Standing Committee of Liturgical Translations of the Archdiocese. He was also an adjunct Professor of Homiletics at Holy Cross Seminary.

He is past President of the Minneapolis Ministerial Association, the Twin Cities Metropolitan Church Commission, the Minneapolis Professional Men's Club, the Minneapolis Kiwanis, and the Greater Minneapolis Council of Churches. He was a member of the Board of the Children's Heart Fund, and is listed in WHO'S WHO in RELIGION 1976-77. He received the WCCO Good Neighbor Award in 1973 and the Alumnus Citation from Holy Cross Seminary.

He retired in January 1993 after serving at St. Mary's for 44 years. He is currently the President of *Light & Life Publishing Company*. He is the author of over 75 books, pamphlets and brochures.

Other titles by Anthony M. Coniaris

Introducing the Orthodox Church
My Daily Orthodox Prayer Book
Making God Real in the Orthodox Christian Home
Knowing God: Life's Highest Purpose
Let's Take A Walk Through Our Orthodox Church
Your Baby's Baptism in the Orthodox Church
Nicene Creed For Young People
Surviving the Loss of a Loved One
God Speaks from the Cross
Christ's Comfort For Those Who Sorrow
Daily Lenten Meditations for Orthodox Christians
Icons Speak Their Message
Eye Cannot Say to the Hand, "I Have No Need Of You"
Getting Ready For Marriage in the Orthodox Church
Philokalia: The Bible of Orthodox Spirituality
The Uniqueness of Eastern Christianity

For more titles by Anthony M. Coniaris,
please see our website at www.light-n-life.com.